Burmese Puppets

Titles in the series

Burmese Puppets

NOEL F. SINGER

SINGAPORE
OXFORD UNIVERSITY PRESS
OXFORD NEW YORK'
1992

Oxford University Press

Oxford New York Toronto
Delhi Bombay Calcutta Madras Karachi
Kuala Lumpur Singapore Hong Kong Tokyo
Nairobi Dar es Salaam Cape Town
Melbourne Auckland
and associated companies in
Berlin Ibadan

Oxford is a trade mark of Oxford University Press

© Oxford University Press Pte. Ltd. 1992

Published in the United States by
Oxford University Press, Inc., New York

ISBN 0 19 588589 9

British Library Cataloguing-in-Publication Data

A catalogue record for this book is available from the British Library

Library of Congress Cataloging-in-Publication Data

Singer, Noel F. (Noel Francis), 1937–
Burmese puppets/Noel F. Singer.
p.   cm.—(Images of Asia)
Includes bibliographical references and index.
ISBN 0-19-588589-9 (hard cover):
1. Puppet theatre—Burma—History. I. Title. II. Series.
PN1978.B85S56   1992
791.5'3'09591—dc20
92-19998
CIP

Printed in Singapore by Kyodo Printing Co. (S) Pte. Ltd.
Published by Oxford University Press Pte. Ltd.,
Unit 221, Ubi Avenue 4, Singapore 1440

To the playwrights, vocalists,
and manipulators of the Burmese puppet theatre

Preface and Acknowledgements

In the 1950s I began collecting articles on puppets published in Burmese magazines, and soon became intrigued by some of the contradictory information provided by various 'authorities'. A favourite but infuriating expression was *shay-ah-kha-ga* (in the old days), which could mean anything from fifty years to five centuries, thus making any attempt at dating impossible. Some information came from totally unexpected sources, such as chronicles, poems, songs, and articles on subjects unconnected with puppetry, but it nevertheless enabled further research and a critical rearrangement of a few of the more puzzling fragments.

Fortunately, the period beginning from the latter half of the nineteenth century provided more empirical information, due in part to the observations of Western writers which were usually accompanied by illustrations. Although a few pieces of the jigsaw have yet to be found, enough survives to give a clearer picture of this art form which dominated the Burmese theatrical world for well over a century.

Several people have helped in the preparation of this book. I should particularly like to thank the following museums for permission to reproduce photographs from their collections: The Dryad Collection, Leicestershire Museums, Arts and Records Service; The Pitt Rivers Museum, Oxford; The Powell-Cotton Museum, Kent; and The Victoria and Albert Museum, London.

I also wish to gratefully acknowledge the encouragement and assistance received from Sylvia E. Lu, who has done so much to promote Burmese art. Special thanks go also to Patricia Herbert of the British Library, to Shwebo Mi Mi Gyi, Hla Thamein, and other Burmese authors too numerous to name, whose fascinating accounts have made this book possible, and to Terence Blackburn for his enthusiasm and unfailing support for the project.

All photographs and illustrations are by the author unless otherwise stated.

Bedfordshire   NOEL F, SINGER
1991

Contents

Introduction

BURMA, which borders both India and China, owes much to these two great civilizations. The earliest recorded inhabitants of Burma were the Pyu and the Mon, who established independent kingdoms in Central and Lower Burma. Following an invasion from Nanchao (Yunnan) in AD 832, control of the area passed from the Pyu to migrants from the north-west area of China, who later came to be known as the Burmese. The newcomers established themselves at Pagan, which was to become famous as a centre for Buddhism until the thirteenth century (and where religious belief still consists of a mixture of *nat* (spirit) worship and Buddhism). Under some of their aggressive rulers they plundered neighbouring kingdoms, the capture of skilled craftsmen being especially prized as part of the spoils.

The Burmese nation is made up of four predominant groups known as the Arakanese, the Mon, the Shan, and the Burmese. These groups coexist with sixty or so ethnic minorities who each have their own cultural traditions. But it was only among the Burmese that the art of puppetry was practised.

Although it cannot yet be established when puppets were first used in Burma, evidence of their existence was first recorded in 1444. During the next 300 years the art gradually matured, presentation becoming of a sufficiently high standard for this form of entertainment to be included as part of the court reception for visiting embassies.

In 1776 itinerant puppet troupes were brought under the control of an official who laid down regulations and engaged outstanding groups to perform at court on a regular basis. Rules had to be rigorously followed by these troupes and those living in the environs of the capital. Subsequently, the art of the puppeteer grew rapidly in stature and was acknowledged to surpass that of the live theatre. Until the 1870s many of the puppets were worked with very few strings and acted merely as a focal point for the vocalist. Audiences came to listen to rather than see a performance.

With the fall of Lower Burma to the British following the wars of 1824 and 1852, some of the traditions which were a product of the old feudal laws began to be discarded. Upper Burma was annexed in 1885 and with the removal of the court central authority ceased. Competition in the theatrical professions intensified and to provide novelty in the puppet theatre more strings were added to puppets and manipulatory skills increased further.

The traditional marionette show is considered to have been at its best between 1820 and 1885, experimentation with new ideas only beginning from the late 1890s. By the 1930s, despite the inclusion of new acts, it could not compete with other forms of entertainment. Although there was a brief revival from the late 1940s, it is doubtful whether a specialized art form such as this can ever regain its nineteenth-century popularity.

This book traces the development of puppetry from the earliest times and notes some of the conflicting information offered by some modern Burmese writers on its history. The lengthy processes of carving and making puppets are explained and the various costumes with which the many characters were adorned described. It also deals with the traditions observed by members of a troupe, which were mainly influenced by the particular brand of Buddhism and spirit worship practised in the country. The world of the vocalist and the manipulator, without whom the puppet is a mere limp ornament, has here been compiled for the first time from various Burmese sources. Finally, the book acknowledges the powerful influence of the puppet theatre and the indelible mark it has left on the dance, crafts, and literature of the country.

Historical Background

AT the height of **its popularity** between 1820 and 1885, the puppet theatre in **Burma was** considered superior to the live theatre, such was **the degree of** skill and expertise exhibited by the puppeteers. The *ah-yoke-kyo-ka* (dance of the stringed ones) was even executed **by dancers at court** and at performances for the common people.

A villain, brought to life by a manipulator and a vocalist, usually fell foul of the audience, many of whom became so emotionally involved in a performance that they no longer saw the strings controlling the menacing figure, and it was not unknown for a man to rush up to the stage and rip it apart. When the heroine suffered at the hands of sadistic tormentors, court ladies and peasant girls alike wept. Being pelted with anything that came to hand was a hazard puppeteers of cruel characters had to endure. On the other hand, the sinuous arms of a sumptuously clad Ahpyodaw (maid of honour) (Colour Plate 1) skilfully performing some of the sixty-four traditional postures delighted the watchers.[1] Some puppets, like the maid of honour, became famous throughout the land and were instantly recognized and much loved by the people.

Whenever a particular troupe appeared during the early part of this century, the audience joined in with the musicians to chant a jingle demanding the appearance of their favourite marionette, Ma Shat Tay:

Ahpyodaw Ma Shat Tay htwet khair par daw lay
Saing saya ma aye pay tee par daw lay
Maid of honour Ma Shat Tay, do come out and dance.
Master of the Orchestra, play, play, play.
A celebrity in its own right, the pert little figure ended its act

[1]Thakin Kodaw Hmaing (c.1920) lists the sixty-four ways of dancing and singing.

by sticking its tongue out at the jubilant crowd who shrieked with delight.

Although the origins of the puppet theatre in Burma are not firmly established, some writers believe that the art came to Burma from India. They quote Buddhist texts which suggest that marionettes were already in use by the time of Gautama (403–483 BC). Others look to China where the puppet tradition goes back over 2,000 years and where three types of puppets were employed: the glove variety, stick puppets, and those worked by strings.[2]

An inscription erected by Htihlaing Min (r. 1084–1112) at the Shwesandaw Pagoda in Prome in 1093 states that his subjects often appeared before him bearing gifts. They came dressed as animals, demons, and gods and danced and sang. Horses trotted and elephants presented him with flowers. It is possible that the movements of these dancers and animals may have been instrumental in the creation of puppets. Although U Wun, a minister for the performing arts during the reign of Pagan Min (r. 1846–53), claimed that marionettes were first introduced during the twelfth century, he does not offer any evidence nor have any puppets been observed in the paintings of the period.

Performances probably began spontaneously among the people, with itinerant troupes travelling around the kingdom. Clearly this form of entertainment was established by the fifteenth century as the Tupayon Pagoda Inscription, set up at Sagaing in 1444 by King Narapadi (r. 1443–69), mentions a group of entertainers he dedicated to the shrine. Among them are listed the earliest known professional *ah-yoke-the* (puppeteers).

In 1484 a sixteen-year-old novice monk named Ratthasara (1468–1529) described in his poem, *Buridat-lingagyipyo*, the world of the *naga* serpents who lived in trees, their movements being said to resemble the curious tripping walk of the *ah-yoke-ka* (dancing puppets). The late Dr Ba Han, scholar and barrister,

[2]Among these writers are Dagon Nat Shin (1959); Zeya (1964); and U Thein Naing (1966).

claimed that 'originally marionettes were manipulated from tree-tops by means of strings', although one would have thought this was extremely precarious (1966). Others believed that they used a small triangular platform built on a framework of seven bamboos, with a curtain at the back behind which the manipulators and vocalists stood.

In 1496, on completion of the Mingalazedi Pagoda at Tadar U, Ratthasara immortalized the festivities in another poem called the *Mingalazedi-mawgun*. Among the pageants were wooden figures which moved. One, in particular, was a large Brahmin astrologer with eyes which rotated and lips which opened to recite prayers. It even read the palms of those brave enough to come near it. Unfortunately, Ratthasara is silent on the technique used to operate it, but it is possible that the figure was either strung and worked by a ventriloquist (an ancient art known in China and India) or else there was someone hidden within.

Ratthasara's final reference to puppets appears in the *Thanwara-pyo*, which he composed some time during 1529 in Lower Burma. The fact that it was observed in another part of the country would indicate that puppetry was already well known.

The *Mahayazawindawgyi* (The Great Chronicle) of 1724 also noted that in 1618, when envoys from Goa, Achin, and Masulipatam arrived at Pegu where Anaukpetlun (r. 1605–28) held court, the entertainments organized for them included 'large and small stringed figures'.

The *In-yon-sar-tan*, a treatise on court rituals and ceremonies of the Nyaungyan Dynasty (1599–1751), lists the procedures to be followed when celebrating the Festival of Lights held each year in October. The organizers were instructed to build nine ornate pavilions of bamboo; four on the left were to be reserved for the men and five on the right for the ladies. Here were staged for three nights *thabin-ah-son* (dancing, singing, music, plays, and a marionette show).

Despite this early documentation, some authors since the 1950s have been stating that the puppet theatre did not come into existence until the reign of Singu (r. 1776–82).[3] It can only be assumed that this belief was partly due to the subject not being properly researched. Others quote the saying *thabin-ah-sa-yoke-thay-ka* (dance and drama began with marionettes) which implies that its creation is lost in antiquity.

Deedok U Ba Cho claimed that the 'early' Burmese were an extremely modest people, and intimate contact between the sexes in public, including dancing, was frowned upon (1951). He declared that when live dramatic performances, which included duets between lovers, were introduced during the latter half of the eighteenth century, 'many eyes could not bear to look at [them]'. He concluded that it was one of the reasons why the marionette theatre reigned supreme for so many years, adding that 'even Burmese modesty cannot take exception to little figures of wood play-acting on the stage'.

Dagon Nat Shin supports Deedok U Ba Cho's view and states (without offering any historical evidence), that as people in the 'old days' were ashamed to be observed dancing in public, wooden puppets were used as a substitute (1959). Only in the eighteenth century were people able to overcome their inhibitions and take part in performances.

This modern belief is at variance with archaeological evidence in the form of seventh-century terracotta plaques found at Waw, near Pegu, which depict dancers. The eleventh-century Shwesandaw Inscription also mentions celebrations at the Burmese capital, Pagan, where songs and dances from 'every city, every country district and every village' could be enjoyed. It was the custom to dedicate a troupe of musicians and dancers to a Buddhist temple by one desiring merit, the central icon being entertained daily in a royal manner with all the rituals employed within the palace, as if it were a living king. Indeed, in the wall paintings and works of art which cover the entire Pagan period (1044–1287), numerous pictures of scantily clad male and voluptuous female dancers can be seen.

The belief also contrasts sharply with the way of life of the

[3]Among them are Deedok U Ba Cho (1951); Khin Myo Chit (1976); and U Min Naing (1979).

period in which the men of the ruling classes were noted for their amours and polygamy was common. As to the reluctance for showing affection between the sexes in public, crowd scenes in the murals of the eighteenth-century Sulamani Temple and the Ananda Okkyaung, together with those within the Nat Htaung Kyaung of the first half of the nineteenth century, show couples caressing each other while they watch men and women dance. The Sulamani paintings, in particular, contain an elegant female dancer clad only in a long trailing skirt. One can only assume that this excess of modesty among some elderly Burmese writers was influenced by Victorian prudery and the Christian Missionary Schools resulting from the country being part of the British Empire from 1885 until 1948.

A further claim is that the art of puppetry was attributable to Myawaddy Wungyi U Sa (1766–1853), a prolific writer who was imprisoned in 1837 by Tharrawaddy (r. 1837–46), and who, to relieve the tedium, is said to have made figures from scraps of cloth and acted out plays.[4] This incident is probably true, but as we have seen, the marionette theatre was already well established by then.

Of all the performing arts, the puppet theatre was the first to be allowed the use of a stage at court, and until 1821 the term *ahmyint-thabin* (raised performance) was applied. *Ahneint-thabin* (low-level performance) identified live actors who were compelled to perform on the ground, although this term did not in any way denigrate them. In a feudal society where rank was all important, it was unthinkable that the socially inferior entertainers should occupy a place higher than the audience, but puppeteers were presumably exempt as they could not be seen. Because they were just over a foot high, and possibly because of poor illumination, it was probably thought sensible to display the marionettes from a height.

Several versions exist on the original size and terms applied to puppets, and as a result it is still impossible to establish a

[4] *The Myanmar Swairson Kyam (Encyclopedia Birmanica)* offers four possible beginnings: (1) Fifteenth century; (2) Reign of Singu (1776–82); (3) Myawaddy Wungyi U Sa; (4) Reign of Pagan Min (1846–53).

precise terminology. Unusually, all modern accounts have ignored the earliest word for a marionette—*ah-yoke*—mentioned in the Tupayon Pagoda Inscription of 1444. Some claim, without offering a source or date, that the stringed figures were originally called *yok-gyi* (large marionettes) because they were over 2 feet high.

The *Shwe-nan-thon-war-haya-abidan*, a work on the meaning of titles and ceremonies of the Konbaung Dynasty (1752–1885), gives a different reason. After the invasion of Thailand in 1767 by Sinbyushin (r. 1763–76), among the captives brought back were court dancers who later performed the *Yama-zat-daw* (*Ramayana*) wearing masks. This type of dancing came to be known as *yoke-gyi* (large marionette) to differentiate it from the actual *yoke-thay* (small marionette) which it resembled in both stylized movements and appearance.

Other sources insist that the correct term for the puppet theatre, which is referred to as *sin* (the word could either mean stage or troupe), was *yoke-son-sin* (troupe which used a variety of puppets). Some troupes were said to have employed large figures, others smaller ones, while a third group performed with a miscellaneous collection. Later, those who used even larger figures came to be known as *yoke-gyi-sin* (troupe which used large puppets). In time, because of the weight of the bigger puppets, smaller ones called *yoke-thay* became more popular.

It is doubtful whether there was any significance in the assortment of sizes employed by some of the later troupes. A reasonable assumption would be that these were simply replacements which the proprietor, in the casual Burmese way, had not considered necessary to match with the existing set. Moreover, the decline of the puppet theatre had begun by 1910 and many companies were beginning to disband. It is possible that the larger marionettes were acquired from some of the less fortunate troupes.

Thabin Wun
(Minister for the Performing Arts)

THE post of an official who organized entertainment for the royal court existed in Burma from the earliest times. Nevertheless, it was not until the reign of Singu (r. 1776–82), an accomplished poet, that a separate ministry was created. The king saw the need to control the growing numbers who were joining these professions, and since the collective term for singing, dancing, music, and marionettes was *thabin*, he instituted the post of Thabin Wun (minister). Although the names of seven incumbents—from 1776 to 1885—are known, only the last three can be assigned to a particular reign. The four whose dates of tenure are in dispute are U Thaw, U Po Phyu, U Khit, and U Nu.[1]

Qualifications required for the earlier incumbents were formidable: a candidate had to be an authority on religious and secular literature, judicial and religious laws, and woodcarving and medicine, and have a knowledge of the performing arts as well as the ability to compose songs and verse. He also had to be adept in astrology, the casting of runes, and other magical pursuits.

The first Thabin Wun, an able administrator, devised a set of rules in 1776 to be observed by singers, dancers, musicians, dramatists, and puppet troupes, all of whom had to be registered. For the puppeteers, he listed twenty-eight characters which were to make up a set, and the correct types of wood used in carving them. He also reorganized the sequence in which some of these figures should appear during the first half of a performance.

Although records are unavailable, it was probably the Thabin

---

[1] None of the Burmese accounts consulted by the author agrees, each claiming that they were appointed by a different king.

Wun who designated as protector of the puppeteers an ancient female tree spirit, variously called the Lamaing Shin Ma or the Thit-thar Shin Ma (The Spirit of Wood) (Colour Plate 2).[2] Unlike the icons of other *nat* figures who are shown wearing a red headband, her colour is black (night) with a silver crescent in front. In her hands she holds peacock feathers, symbols of the sun—the symbolism being that darkness is banished with her light, probably alluding to the all-night marionette performance. The age of the puppet theatre had arrived.

In 1778 Singu built a huge gilded monastery and celebrated the dedication ceremony over several days with a lavish display of military might and novel forms of entertainment. Heading the long list of amusements in the dedicatory inscription were puppet performances. Sadly, his peaceful reign, which was so beneficial to the performing arts, came to an abrupt end. The unruly followers of the Prince of Phaungkar seized the palace while the king was on a pilgrimage and placed their unwilling young master on the throne. Inn Wa, the capital, was given up to plunder for seven days and it is not known whether the Thabin Wun survived the atrocities committed in the name of the new king. The terrified courtiers petitioned the ruthless Prince of Badon, who stepped in and restored order. He also had Singu, Phaungkar, and their families put to death. As Badon Min (r. 1782–1819) he brought stability to the kindgom and patronage of the arts was revived due to the interest displayed by his son Shwetaung Min, the Crown Prince. Although the post of Thabin Wun continued, the name of the new minister is uncertain. He was, however, vested with the power to beat, mutilate, and deport any miscreant connected with his department.[3]

A number of visitors to the country noted the presence and

---

[2]During the second half of the nineteenth century two guardians, inferior in rank to the Lamaing Shin Ma, were added. These were the puppets called Bodaw (nat spirit), and a hermit and were hung flanking the other characters.

[3]The first of the three surviving royal orders on the powers of a Thabin Wun and the rules to be observed by puppeteers were issued on 14 February 1776 (U Thein Naing, 1966), in the early part of Badon Min's reign (U Thaw Zin, 1976), and in 1821 during the reign of Sagaing Min (Dagon Nat Shin, 1959).

popularity of the puppet theatre. Vincentius Sangermano, an Italian priest who arrived in the country in 1783, noted that 'a species of comedy is exhibited with puppets' (1893). In 1795 Michael Symes, an envoy from the Governor-General of India to the Burmese court, was entertained with puppet and theatrical performances (1800). Succeeding embassies observed that music, dancing, and marionettes were always present at state functions and at visits to notables. John Crawfurd, the British Envoy to the Court of Ava in 1827, in particular complained that the dancing girls, puppets, and 'the din of Burmese music was uninterrupted from the moment of our arrival until that of our departure' (1829). By the turn of the nineteenth century, puppetry had clearly become a serious art form, designed primarily with the adult in mind. Emphasis was on the dialogue, which was usually in rhyming verse of four syllables interspersed with lengthy passages of elegant prose.

Badon Min was succeeded by Sagaing Min (r. 1819–37), who continued the tradition of theatrical entertainments which by now had become an integral part of court life, and in 1821 the rules drawn up by the first Thabin Wun were updated by a successor with the king's agreement.[4] He stated that the term *ahmyint-thabin* was to be replaced by *yoke-thay* (small marionette) and that only males were eligible to enter the profession. Performances could only be held for three nights in succession by any one troupe. For the musicians, authority was given to the leader to punish insubordination, irrespective of age, and that apart from the instruments used at court (which were decorated with gilding and glass mosaic) all others had to be plain.

On the construction of the stage, his instructions were that it was to be 3 feet high and 18 feet wide and was to be built of a common kind of bamboo. It was not to face directly into any of the cardinal points and mats for flooring were to be laid beginning from the right. A 10-foot-long strip of white cotton was to be used as a backdrop, leaving a space of 4 feet on each

[4]Variously stated as being either U Khit (Shwe Wair Aye, 1973) or U Thaw (Dagon Nat·Shin, 1959).

side, to be called *min-pauk* (royal doorway), through which the puppets were to be introduced.

The actual 'stage' was to be 3 feet deep, although the platform did extend behind the curtain, this space being reserved for the puppeteers and the marionettes. Only leaves from auspicious plants, and not climbers, were to be placed in three holders to signify forests, and these were to be brought out from under the curtained rail and placed along the stage.

A total of thirty-six characters were to constitute a set, eight puppets now being added to the original twenty-eight. Additional rules insisted that supernatural beings were to be introduced from over the backdrop, and that their feet should not come in contact with the floor. Aquatic creatures were to be shown moving along the stage and never raised above it, and animals had to be brought out through the left *min-pauk*.

On the opening night, the person who hired the troupe was to provide offerings to the spirits, and the proprietor was to be given one silver *mat* (a quarter of a rupee) as a token fee, the remainder to be paid at the conclusion of the performance, together with fruit for the puppeteers and musicians.

Instructions were also given on the sequence in which the characters were to be introduced. A performance was to begin with the destruction of the world and its re-creation, at the end of which the spirit medium was to emerge from the right. Only the two lead vocalists were to sing the ritual songs. Once extracts from the music of the thirty-seven *nat* (spirits) had been played, the puppet was to be removed over the backdrop. It was to be followed by a horse, a monkey, a tiger and his enemy, the elephant, a *garuda* bird and his prey, the dragon, two demons, and finally, an alchemist. Each was to perform its characteristic dance. Those which appeared in pairs made their exit together.

Guidelines were also drawn up for the type of plays to be performed. These were to be based on the 550 *Jataka Tales* (Birth Stories of the Buddha), chronicles, legends of pagodas, and stories from Chiang Mai in Thailand. He stated that the dialogue should not offend the clergy or the court, and that offenders would have either their hand or tongue removed.

Rules were also laid down for the presentation of plays. The Thabin Wun stated that court life should always be depicted correctly in terms of speech, dress, and deportment, and that if two kingdoms were mentioned, the model of the palace belonging to the first should be placed on the right, and the second on the left. The play should always begin with the four ministers of the realm, who were to enter in a dignified manner and converse on the affairs of state. Court music must be played when the king appeared and he was to be seated on his throne before it ended. This puppet should always look dignified and must not at any time be shown in a distressed state.

The Thabin Wun also persuaded Sagaing Min to pass a new law which said that apart from the king, four senior queens, and the heir apparent, all others must pay for a performance. This effectively stopped the numerous members of the royal family and officials using their rank to command free entertainment.

For ordinary citizens, permission had to be sought from the local authority before hiring a troupe, but pagoda and religious festival trustees were exempt. If the puppeteers could not perform on the chosen night because of fire, rain, or a civil disturbance, they were entitled to half the agreed fee.

By 1827 the Thabin Wun was apparently also known by two other titles, although these are not mentioned in Burmese accounts. John Crawfurd, for instance, noted that the Yokethay Wun (Minister for Marionettes), also known as the Zat Wun (Minister for Drama), was a witty elderly Thai, said to be a favourite of Sagaing Min, who 'indulges him in such freedoms as would cost the rest of the courtiers the stocks or the bamboo' (1829).

Before severe bouts of depression overtook Sagaing Min, he was an affable and easygoing monarch. His familiarity with entertainers gave disgruntled citizens the opportunity to bring to his attention crimes perpetrated by those in power. Vocalists from marionette troupes were instructed to hint at, or even mention outright, a particularly sensitive matter during a performance. The characters chosen were usually the clowns, but if it happened to be a particularly serious affair, the king, *nat*, or the hermit figures were used because, as 'sacred' personages, their words carried authority. A cleverly phrased comment usually caught the king's attention. Leaders of the ruling clique at his court realized the potential of the marionette stage for state propaganda and were quick to use it.

In 1837 Sagaing Min was forced to abdicate in favour of his younger brother Tharrawaddy (r. 1837–46), who also took an interest in the theatrical arts. It is possible that the Thabin Wun during his reign was U Nu. He was followed by U Wun when Tharrawaddy was succeeded by his son, Pagan Min (r. 1846–53). The various official records for these last two reigns list celebrations, such as the dedication of royal pagodas and other state functions, at which live performers and the puppeteers predominated.

Among the people, too, the puppet theatre was becoming increasingly popular. For many it was a form of escape from the harsh realities of life. Others eagerly attended shows to savour the exquisite pleasure of hearing artfully worded criticisms against corruption and injustice—a verbal form of protest denied to actors of the period which, in their case, would have merited torture and possible death.[5]

Henry Yule, a member of another mission from the Governor-General of India in 1855, said that 'the puppet plays seem to be even more popular among the Burmese than the live drama' (1858). His opinion was that they were similar to those performed by humans, the only difference being that the plots tended to lean towards the supernatural because of the special effects the little figures could achieve.

It is possible that the custom of presenting packets of pickled tea leaves to friends, when inviting them to a marionette show, originated from this period. The leaves, known as *laphet* (*Elaeodendron orientale*), were mixed with sesame seeds, peanuts, garlic, salt, and oil. It is still considered an aid to prevent drowsiness, and was thus popular at all-night performances.

A puppet show was free, as a Buddhist considers it an act of

[5]This novel system continued to be employed until the end of the dynasty in 1885, but no record exists of any puppeteers being punished.

charity for a person not only to share his good fortune but to bring laughter to his neighbours. Witnessing a performance was an education in itself, with members of the lower classes having the opportunity of hearing the elegant phrases and observing the mannerisms affected by their betters. And although the setting was invariably in mythical Buddhist India, the figures were always dressed in contemporary Burmese clothes. All the stories had a moral, and it was hoped that having seen a performance one was enriched by the homilies delivered by some of the characters, moved by the dialogue, and refreshed by the music and songs. Older members among the audience also came away better informed about current affairs at court.

As Buddhists, the Burmese believed that the human life cycle from birth, childhood to adulthood and old age, was represented in the sequence of events enacted by the marionettes. Like the performance itself, one's life, which is mixed with happiness and sorrow, must one day come to an end.

3

The Puppets

An early set of Burmese marionettes probably consisted of a pair of male and female human figures plus familiar creatures such as the horse, elephant, monkey, and tiger. The puppets would have danced and acted out short scenes from Buddhist stories and folk-tales. In time, the role of the couple grew in importance, and they came to be known as the Mintha (prince) (Plate 1) and Minthamee (princess) (Plate 2).

Until well into the second half of the nineteenth century most of the country, with the exception of settled areas, was a vast jungle. The majority of people believed—and still do—that the animals share their habitat with demons and the creatures of the night. Taking advantage of this belief, the puppeteers introduced plots in which the hero and heroine undertook journeys through forests, where they had interesting encounters with its denizens.

Although the number of marionettes decreed by the first Thabin Wun was twenty-eight, there is no evidence to suggest that all the characters were his own creation as some writers would have us believe.[1] It is possible that he simply improved a minor art form which had been in existence for centuries. His stipulation that only this number was to be used could not have been enforced for long either, as most troupes found it impossible to keep to a set number as the plays in their repertoire increased.

A list of figures kept by a touring group prior to the Thabin Wun's reorganization of the marionette stage may have consisted of the following eighteen puppets (Plate 3):[2]

[1] Among them are Deedok U Ba Cho (1951); Khin Myo Chit (1976); and Pantanaw Win Thein (c.1970).

[2] The illustrations in Plate 3 are conjectural, and are based on seventeenth-century wall paintings in the Phowintaung Caves, Monywa, Upper Burma. As puppets mimicked live actors they, too, would have been dressed in the fashion of the day.

1. Mintha (prince). Late nineteenth century.

2. Minthamee (princess). Late nineteenth century. (Courtesy of the Trustees of the Victoria and Albert Museum)

Mythological

1. Belu (demon).
2. Zawgyi (alchemist).
3. Naga (dragon).
4. Galon (garuda).
5. Byarmar (Brahma).

Animal

6. Myin (horse).
7. Sin-phyu (white elephant).
8. Sin-net (black elephant).
9. Myauk (monkey).
10. Kyar (tiger).
11. Kyet-to-yway (parrot).

Human

12. Natkadaw (spirit medium).
13. Mintha (prince).
14. Minthamee (princess).
15. Bayin (king).
16. Wun (minister).
17. Ponna (Brahmin astrologer, villain).
18. Yathay (hermit).

Since the stories were mostly set at court and in the forest, these eighteen characters would probably have been adequate for all situations.

The list of twenty-eight puppets claimed to have been created by the Thabin Wun in 1776 consisted of the following:

Mythological

1. Belu (demon with green face).
2. Belu (demon with green face).
3. Zawgyi (alchemist).
4. Naga (dragon).
5. Byarmar (Brahma).
6. Nat (spirit).

Belu (demon)   Zawgyi (alchemist)   Naga (dragon)

Galon (garuda)   Byarmar (Brahma)

Mythological Puppets

3. The eighteen puppets kept by an itinerant troupe prior to 1776. The drawings, although conjectural, are based on seventeenth-century wall paintings in the Phowintaung Caves, Monywa, Upper Burma.

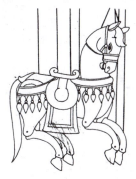

Myin (horse)

Sin-phyu (white elephant)

Sin-net (black elephant)

Myauk (monkey)

Kyar (tiger)

Kyet-to-yway (parrot)

Animal Puppets

19

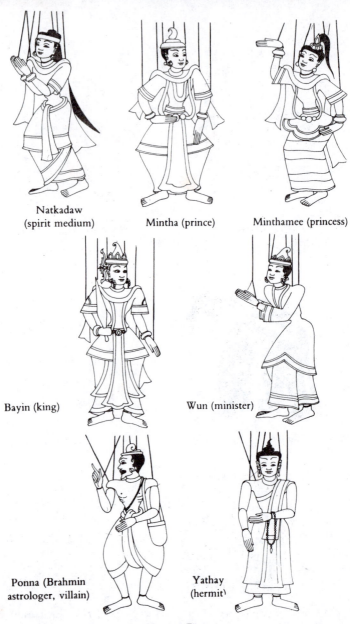

Natkadaw
(spirit medium)

Mintha (prince)

Minthamee (princess)

Bayin (king)

Wun (minister)

Ponna (Brahmin
astrologer, villain)

Yathay
(hermit)

Human Puppets

1. Ahpyodaw (maid of honour). *c.*1880.

2. Lamaing Shin Ma, guardian spirit of puppeteers. *c.*1880.

8. Two ministers. *c*.1880. The one with the red face always plays the role of the villain.

4. Head of a male figure with turban showing typical painted features. Late nineteenth century.

5. Head of a Mintha (prince) showing the painted skin folds on the neck. Late nineteenth century.

6. Male figure showing the neck disk which joins the head to the torso.

7. Lu-shwin-daw (clown). *c.*1880.

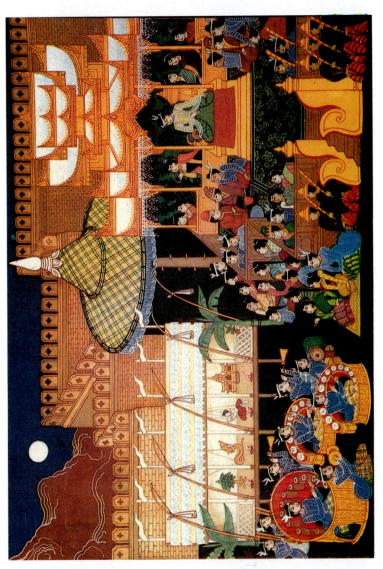

8. A performance of the *maha-sin-daw-gyi* (state troupe) within the Mandalay Palace. Painting by the author.

9. *Win-sin* troupe performing in Mandalay. *c.* 1869. Painting from a parabaik (folded paper book). (Courtesy of the Trustees of the Victoria and Albert Museum)

11. Myauk (monkey). *c.*1880.

10. *Ah-yat-sin* (itinerant troupe). *c.*1900.

12. Belu (demon) holding on to a long
staff. *c.*1850.

13. Belu (demon) holding two short
staves. *c.*1850.

14. Zawgyi (alchemist). *c.*1880.

15. Thu-nge-daw (page boy). Late nineteenth century.

16. Mintha (prince), modern puppet. (Courtesy of Sylvia E. Lu)

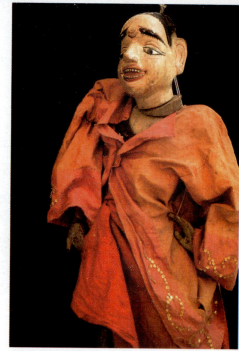

17. Clown, modern puppet. (Courtesy of Sylvia E. Lu)

18. Modern puppets in Mandalay. (Courtesy of Sylvia E. Lu)

19. Mintha (prince) fighting a belu (demon). Lacquer panel with characters from the puppet stage. *c*.1830.

20. Scene from a *kalaga* (applique hanging) showing Ma Mai U being carried off by a tiger. *c*.1900.

Animal

  7. Myin (horse).
  8. Sin-phyu (white elephant)
  9. Sin-net (black elephant).
10. Myauk (monkey).
11. Kyar (tiger).
12. Kyet-to-yway (parrot).

Human

13. Natkadaw (spirit medium).
14. Ahpyodaw (maid of honour).
15. Mintha (prince).
16. Minthamee (princess).
17. Bayin (king).
18.–21. Wun-gyi-lay-bar (four ministers, two of whom are depicted with a red face and two with white).
22. Minthagyi (senior prince with a red face).
23. Minthagyi (senior prince with a white face).
24. Ponna (Brahmin astrologer, villain)
25. Yathay (hermit).
26. Ah-may-oh (old lady).
27.–28. Lu-shwin-daw (two clownish attendants).

The number was decided by the Thabin Wun as symbolic of the twenty-eight attributes which made up the human body, as mentioned in the *Abhidhamma-pitaka*, a work on the psychological and metaphysical aspects of Buddhism, and each character had to be interpreted accordingly. Although this may have been relevant to the intellectuals at court, by the 1880s the symbolism of the figures was beginning to lose its meaning, and the audience merely wished to be entertained.

It is said that a complete set of characters from the *Ramayana* was also kept by the court troupe, but this is doubtful as no record of this has been discovered. If the claim is correct, the number of figures would have been enormous. However, highlights from this popular epic were no doubt included, and a small group of the principal characters specially made for it.

This epic, which was the preserve of the live theatre, is known to have taken forty-five nights to perform.

One particular character, known as the Than-cho-kaing (Holder of the Sweet Voice), does not appear in the original list of puppets, indicating that it was introduced at a later date. Although famous troupes maintained a separate puppet for the Than-cho-kaing, from about the 1860s the poorer companies used one of the two clowns. The figure, worked only by the most experienced vocalist, performed at receptions where 'it' composed flattering descriptions of eminent people who were present. On stage it gave recitals and narrated parts of the play. However, this character, which was much appreciated by the more refined audiences of the nineteenth century, became redundant during the 1920s.

Some of the plays featured Kinnaras (half human half bird-like creatures from Hindu mythology, but adapted to Burmese taste). These strange beings are usually depicted in their original hybrid form in paintings, carvings, and terracotta, but their role in a puppet play was always taken by one of the human puppets with wings attached either to the hips or the wrists.

Although puppet characters began to alter from the 1820s onwards, the demon, alchemist, horse, elephant, monkey, tiger, spirit medium, prince, princess, king, minister, and hermit remained constant. In keeping with the tendency of the early Burmese to preserve *hton-san* (tradition), it is possible that these figures were retained because they were the original 'cast' used by troupes in the distant past. Until the late 1890s part of the dance sequence of the Ahpyodaw consisted of impersonating them. Writers on the history of marionettes have not given a reason why this particular character was chosen to perform these set pieces. Perhaps being the first puppet to appear on the second and third nights of the performance, it was hoped that the gestures would serve as a reminder and as a tribute to those earlier figures, and also as a preview of the delightful characters to follow. Unfortunately, the correct order in which they were played was disregarded by many troupes. Among the new characters which were introduced was the incongruous and

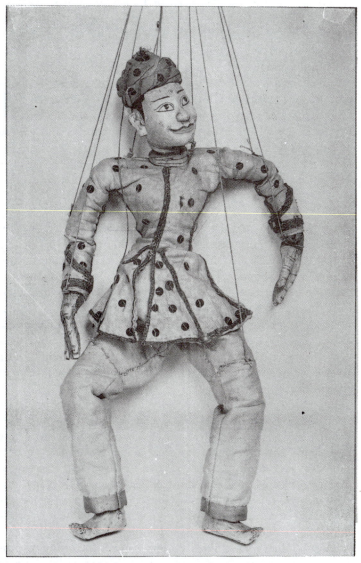

4. **Seik-kala (Indian syce), a comic figure. Late nineteenth century. (Courtesy of the Trustees of the Victoria and Albert Museum)**

clownish figure of the Saik-kala or Indian syce (Plate 4). This figure was invented by a puppeteer from British Burma, and represents one of the servants without whom life was intolerable for a newly arrived colonial.

With the annexation of Upper Burma by the British in 1885, the livelihood of thousands of people who depended on court patronage was thrown into turmoil. As a result, each professional group went its own way and the fight for survival began. In a bid to remain competitive, the number and variety of puppets increased still further from the late 1890s, many characters being borrowed from the live theatre.

How Puppets were Made

Arists who decorated the interiors of temples with scenes from religious and secular stories were probably those same people called upon to paint marionettes. One may visualize early examples of puppets through studying murals from the appropriate periods as painters from each century had their own distinctive style. Unfortunately, as conservation was quite unknown among the Burmese, the oldest marionettes in existence only date from the second half of the nineteenth century, and are likely to be found in foreign collections. Those that have survived in Burma have been repainted beyond recognition.

Puppets were not made by professional woodcarvers but by specialists who produced the complete character: that is, they painted, costumed, and strung it. During the latter half of the nineteenth century one such specialist, U Pho Che, a master puppet maker of Taungdwingyi, was renowned for the exquisite faces of his Mintha and Minthamee characters. U Yar Kyaw was known for his villains, while U Hman Yaung for the humorous faces of his clowns. Nevertheless, a few versatile puppeteers are known to have made their own.

In 1855 Henry Yule noted during his visit to Burma that the size of the puppets varied from 10 to 15 inches (1858). It could be that because the small size had long been a strain on the eyes, the Thabin Wun decreed that marionettes used by the court troupe be increased to 27 inches and figures for other companies to 22 inches. The author U Thein Naing has said that the ruling applied to the principal characters only; the size of the remainder is not known (1966). Unfortunately, neither he nor other sources offer a precise date when this came into effect. But the writer George Scott (Shway Yoe), who arrived in the country in 1879, said that the puppets were 'frequently as much as 2 or 3 feet high' (1896). It is therefore possible that the change in size occurred soon after the court moved from the former capital Amarapura to the new one at Mandalay in 1857. Many of the puppets to have survived from the second half of the nineteenth century usually conform to these two stated sizes.

A human puppet comprised the head, upper torso, arms, forearms and hands, lower torso, thighs, legs, and feet (Plate 5). The torso, made in two sections, was joined at the waist by a thin cloth sheath. If a male figure had to change roles, it could only do so as another male.

The original instructions on the use of the correct kind of wood for each puppet were issued by the first Thabin Wun after consulting works on astrology and divination which contain advice on the compatibility of species of trees with humans born on a particular day of the week. *Yamane* (Clogwood), being rare, was reserved for the principal human characters, including the horse and *nat*. *Ayegayit* (*Millingtonia hortensis*) was used for the hermit, king, and the four ministers. Other characters were made from *ma-u* (*Anthocephalus cadamba*) or *panmairsar* (*Albizia stipulata*). In 1821 this list was amended, although *yamane* was retained, the remaining three being replaced by *letpan* (*Bombax malabaricum*) or *thanat* (*Garcinia elliptica*). Other lists are also known, but these date from the late nineteenth century and are often confused and inconsistent.

When the required wood was obtained, a piece was placed in water. The side that surfaced was considered female while the immersed side was considered male. Characters were carved accordingly, complete with the appropriate sex organ. It is

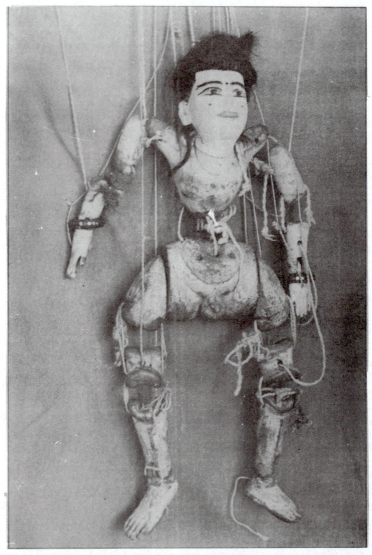

5. A nineteenth-century Mintha from the Myodaw Thein Aung Troupe, near Myingyan. Face recently repainted. Claimed to have been once strung with sixty strings.

difficult to believe that these instructions were strictly followed for long outside the capital, and once the power of the Thabin Wun waned the craftsmen probably used whatever soft wood was available.

The limbs were painted white with either *hton* (chalk) or *myai-phyu* (limestone) and the resin of the *tammar* (*Azadirachta indica*).[3] Powdered *kankusan* (steatite) mixed with a liquid in which the kernel of roasted tamarind seeds (*Tamarindus indica*) had been boiled, was used exclusively for the face. This was applied layer by layer; eight to ten coats were not unknown. If the correct sequence was not followed, the surface cracked and could not be repaired. This time-consuming process produced an almost porcelain-like texture which was non-reflective and did not crack. A padded bag was then used to protect the head.

Unlike the glove puppets of Fujian (Fukien), in China, where colour on the face of a character signified a particular personality, only five such figures are known in Burmese marionette tradition. The senior prince and two ministers (Colour Plate 3) were originally depicted with red faces, although this changed to a paler version from the second half of the nineteenth century. The colour supposedly represented malevolence, but other villains, such as the Brahmin astrologer and the witch, have white faces. The original meaning of red has now been lost as has the significance of green on the two demons. A troupe in the 1960s, for instance, was observed using a pair with gilded faces. It is possible that the association of some characters with a particular colour may have originated from the Hun Luang or royal puppets of Thailand.

Features were first outlined with *hinthapada* (red oxide of mercury) and later completed in black, which was obtained by mixing soot with *tammar* resin and the gall of the *ngagyin* fish (*Cirrhina morigala*) (Colour Plates 4 and 5). Eyes were painted in, although by the 1890s flat porcelain pieces, originally intended for the Buddha image trade, became popular. Some of the principal characters had pupils of *mahuya* (agate), but this

[3]Despite being brown-skinned, Burmese artists usually depict members of their race, supernatural beings, and Buddha with a white skin.

was rare and was probably a late nineteenth-century indulgence.

Great care was taken with the face as it had to portray both joy and grief. The latter emotion could be achieved by raising the hand of the puppet and covering its smiling mouth. The slightly knitted eyebrows then portrayed a look of anguish.

Prior to about 1920, the human face was carved in one piece, without any movable parts, but soon some puppet makers began producing heads using the same technique as a ventriloquist's dummy from the West. This innovation, however, was reserved for the secondary characters who 'spoke' the most, such as the clowns. The lead figures, admired for their *ah-hla* (beauty), continued to be carved in the traditional manner, with a smile fixed on their smooth faces and without the disfiguring joins running down the corners of the lips to the chin that characterized some of the secondary characters. Until the turn of this century, facial decoration, consisting of dots and lines in gold ink and red, was popular. The designs were even copied to 'beautify' young children and boys taking part in Buddhist rituals, one of these being the *shin-pyu* ceremony where a boy is dressed up in elaborate robes and taken in procession to a monastery. On arrival his hair is shaved and as a novice he spends a few weeks being instructed in the Buddhist scriptures.

The heads of the Mintha, Minthamee, and a few others were thickly studded with long strands of hair secured by tiny slivers of bamboo held in place with lacquer (see Plates 6 and 8). Only human hair could be used. The heads of lesser characters were carved with a hair knot. Minthamee figures originally wore their hair hanging loose down the back, but from the second half of the nineteenth century many affected the *byar-pa-san* style, which consisted of a short length of hair combed out from the temple in a crescent behind each ear, with the rest being gathered in a long pony-tail. This was replaced in the 1890s by elaborately coiled styles decorated with numerous hairpins and flowers.

When tragedy struck the hero and heroine during a performance, their hair would be deliberately undone, this being the traditional sign of distress, and in this dishevelled state they underwent torment with much beating of breasts. Special songs, known as *ngo-chin* (weeping songs), were sung at such moments. The carefully chosen words and pathetic movements of the figures, combined with the heart-rending sounds from the orchestra, had a devastating effect on the audience, many of whom enjoyed a good cry.

The head and short neck of a puppet were joined to the upper torso by a circular piece of wood called a *lair-san-chat*, which was thick in front but sloping towards the back (Colour Plate 6). A string, fixed to the neck, passed through it and into the base of the head. Four red lines, two on the neck and two on the disc, represented the much admired skin folds usually seen on plump people.

Until the latter half of the nineteenth century, a pagoda-shaped crown or helmet was carved in one piece as the head, and was ornamented with gilding and glass mosaic. Astute puppeteers realized that if the head-dress was made in segments, sections could either be added or removed so that the role of the puppet could be changed.

Almost all the marionettes were stored in a *htan-khauk-phar*, a container made from the leaves of the *htan* or toddy palm (*Borassus flabelliformis*), although large circular bamboo baskets were also used. These were replaced in modern times by tin trunks and wooden boxes. The tradition that puppets must not be touched with the feet still persists, and that characters which are natural enemies are never stored together.

Animals, such as the horse, tiger, and elephant were always carried prominently so that they could be seen. The Burmese love performances of all kinds, and the excitement caused in a village by the arrival of a troupe bearing puppets can well be imagined.

The Costumes

The *Mani-yadana-pon-kyam*, a collection of parables and historical incidents compiled by Shin Sandalinka in 1781, states that during the reign of Min Gyi Nyo (r. 1485–1530) a villager was charged with tricking the king's preceptor by claiming he was Thagyar Min (Indra). He created this illusion by appearing at sunset in a fantastic robe decorated with the iridescent wing cases of insects. It could be that some of the costumes worn by the poorer class of itinerant dancers were also ornamented in a similar manner. As the supply was readily available, there is a possibility that puppeteers also used these to embellish their little figures. The most common insect was the *po-hmin-taung* or chameleon beetle (*Buprestis sp*), the golden green wings of which were employed to ornament palm leaf fans and even one of the jewelled gold crowns worn by Mindon (r. 1853–78) and Theebaw (r. 1878–85). Sequins were imported from India from about the seventeenth century, but craftsmen employed by the Shwe-taik (Treasury) also struck huge amounts of sequins for the robes of the royal family and officials. Two types, one flat and the other cupped, were made from gold and silver foil, while gilt metal was used for other decorations.

The costume of a Minthamee (Plate 6) from the second half of the nineteenth century, which is now in the Victoria and Albert Museum, London, consists of a breast cloth over which is worn a long-sleeved jacket, open in front and decorated with flat sequins. From the waist down the jacket flares out into two crescent shapes which, stiffened with thin pieces of bamboo, stand out from each side of the hips. The pattern on the puppet's *htamein* (skirt) is picked out with imported coloured braid and sequins. This was in imitation of a ceremonial garment called *keik htamein* which was worn by high-ranking queens and princesses and consisted of thin gold discs embossed with various designs and set with jewels sewn on to the material.

Originally a piece of cloth known as *ahnar* would have been attached to the bottom of the skirt worn by the puppet, as is shown on the Minthamee in Plate 7. For centuries fashion decreed that upper-class ladies should adorn themselves in long trailing skirts. This was always sewn in two pieces, the top part being of a richly woven material, while the bottom, beginning

6. Minthamee (princess) in typical costume. Late nineteenth century. (**Courtesy** of the Trustees of the Victoria and Albert Museum)

7. Minthamee (princess) with typical ornamentation. Late nineteenth century. (Courtesy of the Pitt Rivers Museum)

from just above the ankles, being of a slightly coarser cloth which could be removed for washing. On the wrists of the puppet are a pair of large bangles made of rolled cotton covered with tinsel and sequins. Long looped strands composed of imitation pearls called *mok padee*, together with beads, tiny shells, and glass jewels would have adorned its neck (see Plate 7). These embellishments first appeared on Minthamee puppets which, being small, could be lavishly decorated by the owner. Actresses and female dancers soon copied the style. The now dishevelled hair of the marionette would originally have been tied with a ribbon.

The Mintha (Plate 8) is also dressed in a long-sleeved, tight-fitting jacket, but without an opening in front. It, too, is designed so that it flares out from the hips. The *pasoe* (sarong) is made to look more voluminous than the one worn by the Minthamee.

By the 1890s, because of the availability of accessories from abroad, costumes for the principal characters were more lavishly ornamented. The chest, arms, and shoulders of the Mintha and Minthamee, in particular, were covered with thick clusters of imitation gems which flashed in the lamplight.

Before 1890 each human figure was recognizable by the design of its costume, which was seldom changed. If the story required the metamorphosis of the Minthamee into an alchemist, the puppet simply slipped into its new role still dressed in its original costume, but assumed the posture and mannerisms associated with the alchemist character. The orchestra also assisted by playing its special tune. In the eyes of the audience, the princess had indeed been transformed into the flamboyant Zawgyi.

The Strings

The *kyo* (strings) which worked the marionettes had to be strong. Should one snap during a performance, the troupe not only lost face but considered it a bad omen. If performing at court, the unlucky man was liable to be thrashed.

8. Mintha (prince) in typical costume. Late nineteenth century. (Courtesy of the Trustees of the Victoria and Albert Museum)

Some authorities maintain that early puppets were manipulated with few strings, the most being six. However, by 1830 at least one figure was seen to have been strung with thirty-two strings. This was noted by a Captain Pemberton who stated that the marionette was about 1 foot high and was extremely lifelike (1960). He was also informed that the puppeteers 'had another as large as life, which was just now out of order, but that with a properly prepared stage, on which the man was concealed, the illusion was perfect'. These marionettes must have been rare examples since few other Westerners before 1880 mentioned the unusually high number of strings or the large size of the puppets they observed.

The pair of marionettes in the Victoria and Albert Museum (see Plates 6 and 8) appear to have only five strings: the central one, which took the weight of the figure, and one for each wrist and elbow. On closer inspection, it was found that the two important ones, on each temple, were missing.

The men responsible for introducing mobility to the lower parts of puppets are believed to be U Phon Mo, vocalist for the Mintha, and his assistant, Ko Lun Tar. No dates are available, but as the former is included in the list of leading Mintha for the reign of Theebaw one can only assign it to this innovative period when, after the long dreary reign of the religiously inclined Mindon, the young royals who ruled in Mandalay demanded a livelier form of entertainment. The days when many of the court puppets stood and recited lengthy passages from the *Jataka Tales,* with occasional languid movements, were over. Mobility was in demand, and the Mintha and Minthamee now sang the latest love songs and danced for nearly two hours.

By the 1900s a human figure was divided into three sections with eighteen strings attached to the appropriate parts:

Top: Temples (2) making the head nod and move, a distinctive feature of Burmese puppets; back (2), where strong twine took the weight of the marionette; shoulders (2); elbows (2); back of the hand (2). A metal hook in the palms of the Mintha and Minthamee enabled the figures to lift parts of their costume when dancing. Others had fingers made in segments which could be folded to hold an instrument.

Middle: Hips (2).

Lower: Knees (2); heels (2); toes (2).

All eighteen strings, each about 4 inches long and called *ah-se-kyo* (primary string), were permanently fixed. To these were tied the longer secondary ones, a necessary system as costumes had to be changed.[4] When the troupe rested, the long strings were removed and the puppets stored away.

The top and middle strings were hooked on to a *dalet* (a handle usually shaped like a bird in flight) (Plate 9). Occasionally a second one took those from the lower section of the puppet. The manipulator then operated from two *dalet*, using the strings individually as required.

Prior to 1913 a Minthamee puppet was unable to perform life-like movements, such as placing ornaments in its hair. But during that year, a female dancer called Ma Sein Thon became famous for her ability to move various parts of her anatomy independently to music; her gestures are believed to have shocked some and delighted others. U Htun Win, a talented and inventive puppet maker, is said to have developed a marionette which could imitate the movements of the young lady. The outcome culminated in the pair appearing together in special shows. The new model, which had more strings than the Mintha, became popular and was said to have been copied by other famous troupes.

Competition spurred some puppeteers into producing some amazing effects. For instance, the head of a witch could be detached, made to float away to another part of the stage, and then brought back to rejoin its body. In the gruesome play *Hti Lat Po U*, a villain could rip open the belly of his pregnant lover and remove the foetus for magical purposes. A juggler could also perform incredible feats with hoops and spheres.

Writers on puppets, Burmese and foreign, have often fallen prey to the much-quoted myth about nineteenth-century

---

[4]Some manipulators have been known to count both sets of strings, thereby doubling the number on a puppet.

9. Mintha (prince) with the strings hooked on to a *dalet* (handle). Late nineteenth century. (Courtesy of the Pitt Rivers Museum)

puppeteers being able to work figures with as many as sixty strings.[5] The last known example is said to have been owned by a U Win of Myingyan, in 1933, a mysterious figure who cannot now be traced. However, without documentation these claims are difficult to accept, and readers knowledgeable about puppets will question the feasibility of manipulating a figure with so many strings. Apart from the Mintha and Minthamee, which may have at the most twenty strings, the rest were worked by between two and eighteen. It could be that U Win's puppet had only thirty primary strings, but he decided to count the secondary ones as well and thus reached an impressive total.

U Thein Naing, while researching for his book on marionettes, said that he had counted forty-five strings on the figure of a Minthamee used by U Paw Shein of Mandalay (1966). Its claim to fame was the ability to dance with a lighted candle. He also said that the high number of strings—as many as eighty—recorded in some accounts were the fabrications of puppeteers and writers with an urge to impress.

[5]The owner of the Myodaw Thein Aung Troupe, near Myingyan, whose puppet is illustrated in Plate 5, claims that the figure was once strung with sixty strings.

4
A Puppet Troupe

A company was composed of both seasoned performers and apprentices and sometimes additional professionals were hired. Stage personnel, known as *shay-lu* (front people), invariably consisted of three principal vocalists, two manipulators who only worked the Mintha, Minthamee, and the Zawgyi, five manipulators who doubled as vocalists for the minor characters, and a *sin-htein* (keeper of the stage and puppets). All were considered senior to the musicians, who were merely *nauk-lu* (followers).

By the second half of the nineteenth century the proprietor of a troupe was usually the vocalist for the Mintha or the Minthamee. Hla Thamein states that the fee for a performance was 100 rupees, but fails to give a date when this was the standard charge (1968). The money was divided between the professionals and the apprentices: the first received 60 rupees, which was further subdivided between themselves, and the second group had the remainder.

A troupe was initially known by the name of its town or village. But as the role of the lead vocalist increased, his name superseded it—a trend believed to have begun at Mandalay during the 1870s.

It was not unknown for the entire company, including the musicians, to live together in one huge *waing* (compound) owned by the proprietor. There they rested and rehearsed during the monsoon, from about May to September, and lived off the earnings of the previous season.

The Vocalists (Ah-so)

Although the Tupayon Pagoda Inscription of 1444 lists the members of a puppet troupe, their roles were not defined. As a result, the names of vocalists prior to the nineteenth century are unknown. Currently, the earliest appears to be Saya Shwe Yae of Kyaukkar village, Upper Burma, who performed at the capital from about 1819.

A vocalist was senior to a manipulator because, no matter how cleverly the latter worked his puppet, it was the voice that held the audience's attention. Describing a person or scene could take several minutes, during which the most extravagant comparisons were made. Each word was played with, caressed, or emphasized, depending on the mood of the moment. Many vocalists had such retentive memories that they were able to work without the aid of a script, and their strong voices could rise above the shrill music. They often prefixed their name with that of the character they portrayed, such as *Yoke-thay Mintha* U Thar Pyaw or *Yoke-thay Minthamee* U Chin Taung. Troupes where both principals were equally famous were unknown, as one would insist on assuming the dominant role. This meant that the other, if talented, would leave and form his own group.

A successful vocalist had to be adept in a number of areas:

Ah-pyaw: Delivery of the dialogue in a convincing manner, a knowledge of poetry, and the ability to introduce extracts from religious and secular works at appropriate moments.

Ah-so: Different methods of singing.

Ah-ngo: Crying and singing dirge-like 'weeping songs' during moments of distress—the highlight of most plays.

Ah-chau: Using words in an artful, coaxing manner to play on the emotions of the audience.

Due to a regrettable Burmese Buddhist belief concerning the 'weaker' sex, women were once forbidden to step on to the stage because their presence would have 'defiled' it.[1] As a result, all the female roles were taken by men. Another

---

[1] A Burman insists that only a man can become a Buddha, and consider females lower than a male dog—an unfortunate lapse in an otherwise compassionate religion—and to this day a woman's presence in certain parts of a stupa is not tolerated. This can be seen at the Shwe Dagon Pagoda in Rangoon where women, although permitted the use of the main platform, are denied access to the lower terrace of the stupa.

explanation is that the early puppeteers also felt vulnerable during a show, and had no wish to be distracted by the presence of ladies. However, the late Maung Htin Aung believed that the practice of banning females from the marionette stage 'may have been only an attempt by men to reserve the profession for themselves' (1956).

The role of the Minthamee was particularly demanding for a man as there was a complex range of scales to be mastered and each song had to be sung in a special way. The speech and mannerisms used by upper-class ladies were studiously observed to ensure authenticity during a performance. The vocalist also had to be proficient in the twelve basic feminine roles: that of a coquette; that of a woman in travail; knowing how to address each character (an accomplishment in a feudal society); pining for a lover or child; playing a tragic role; changing into another character; fighting verbally for a loved one; metamorphosing into a demon, yet retaining human emotions; expressing great suffering, resulting in a mental breakdown; being struck dumb (and communicating such a state with expressive actions); playing a tragic mother ordered to kill her child; and dying convincingly (the character was either brought back to life or became a good spirit).

Henry Yule observed that 'much of the dialogue was always in singing, and in those parts the attitudes, action, and sustained wailings, has a savour of the Italian opera and was intensely comical at first' (1858). The writer George Scott (Shway Yoe) was equally amazed at the accuracy with which the female voice was imitated, and at the elocutionary powers of the vocalists and the great feeling with which songs were sung (1896). After witnessing several shows, he said that he could understand the national preference for the puppet theatre.

The femininity of their roles did not intrude into the private lives of these Minthamee vocalists for many were happily married men. Some of the more celebrated were highly educated, or had been actors in their youth. They would often compose songs or wittily improvise during a show, a gift which the audience appreciated. Many had their own following of dedicated fans who sat near the stage to note down any new material. Composers from less famous troupes often joined these little bands, with mercenary plagiaristic intent. As they grew older, younger members in the profession used the word *ahmay* (mother) out of respect when addressing them.

During a performance the vocalist sat near the manipulator (Plate 10). The musicians also took their cue from him. The moment a puppet was lowered on to the stage, the vocalist's vast store of knowledge was instantly unleashed, and the appropriate section faultlessly recited.

Next in importance to the Minthamee vocalist was the vocalist for the Lu-shwin-daw (clown) (Colour Plate 7). He enjoyed the privilege of moving in and out of the play, and sometimes gave a commentary on the proceedings. Indeed, he was one of the few figures who could criticize the behaviour and follies of the highest in the land; only Buddha escaped his sarcastic tongue.

During the reign of Mindon the most famous Mintha vocalist was U Thar Pyaw. The monarch, who happened to hear him, was so impressed that he commanded him to join the ranks of the court puppeteers. He also appointed him Thabin Wun, thus replacing U Wun, the previous incumbent under the deposed Pagan Min. Among the privileges which went with the post was the warrant to wear a *tho-yin-eingyi* (white court robe), to carry a sword with a scabbard of embossed silver, and to be shaded by a gold umbrella. Two attendants, each holding a red lacquer wand to which a white scarf had been tied, proceeded him.

U Thar Pyaw soon became the king's favourite, and often broke his own department's rule by improvising during a royal performance, an action which had been forbidden by a previous Thabin Wun. Puppeteers who were late for a performance were punished not by him, but by the Lord Mayor, and it is on record that U Thar Pyaw had leg irons placed on him for this offence. When Mindon arrived at the theatre, he was confronted by the shackled figure of the little Mintha, hopping back and forth across the stage to a song lamenting the Thabin Wun's

10. Manipulator, vocalist, and puppet. *c.*1870.

predicament. The king immediately ordered his release.

Because of U Thar Pyaw's position at court, whenever he performed beyond the confines of the palace, the stage was decorated with a pair of royal *yaza-mat* (bamboo fences), his ministerial gold umbrella, two red wands, and a banana tree in fruit.

On the accession of Theebaw, U Thar Pyaw was replaced by U Chin Taung, a Minthamee vocalist, composer, and great humorist. He was also the last person to hold this office. It is interesting to note that the Thabin Wun appointed by Mindon was the vocalist for the Mintha (male) whereas the appointee during Theebaw's reign was that of a Minthamee (female). Perhaps this was because Mindon was very much the master of his house, whereas poor Theebaw and his weak court were ruled by his domineering Queen Suphayarlat, who is claimed to have said that trousers made a good dress for women, and very nearly succeeded in replacing the graceful *htamein* (skirt) of her unwilling ladies with them.

It is recorded that U Chin Taung had a rival called U Thar Dun Aung, a Mintha vocalist, who never missed an opportunity to make scurrilous remarks and compose slanderous songs about the object of his envy. It is not known whether the Thabin Wun was extremely good-natured or whether the post had by now lost its authority, for earlier incumbents would not have tolerated such insolence. Finally, the miscreant was summoned before Queen Suphayarlat who demanded a public apology, accompanied by the obligatory tray of offerings for her favourite.

Saya Pu (Plate 11), a young vocalist with an unrivalled singing voice, soon replaced U Chin Taung and became the prima donna of the marionette stage during the heady days of Theebaw's rule. His puppet, from whom he was inseparable, was called Pu Pu (Mistress Petite). Saya Pu's troupe was still enjoying great popularity until 1908, when Saya Pu was arrested by the colonial powers for writing a patriotic song about the Burmese kings which they considered subversive. He died six years later cradling the little figure of Pu Pu.

11. The celebrated Minthamee vocalist, Saya Pu (1860–1914).

The Manipulators (Kyo-swair)

In most cultures the jerky movements of puppets are accepted by the audience as being unavoidable, and the manipulators thus make no attempt to produce lifelike gestures. Burmese puppeteers, however, from the second half of the nineteenth century onwards, succeeded in imitating human mannerisms with considerable success. Although the fame of a troupe usually depended on the lead vocalists, occasionally it was the skill of its *kyo-swair* which drew the crowds. In some troupes a Mintha or Minthamee vocalist was able to do both, but this was extremely exhausting and was only exhibited occasionally for scenes such as the all-important duet between the prince and the princess.

An apprentice stayed with a troupe for several years, during which time—depending on his personal circumstances—he was usually fed by the owner and took his turn with household duties. A talented young man was often encouraged to marry into the family. Dagon Nat Shin claims that a training period of twenty to twenty-five years was not unknown for either vocalist or manipulator (1959). This appears to be an excessively long time and may have applied only to some individuals who had difficulty in mastering the art.

Instruction during the first two years was concentrated on the animals and secondary characters. The dragon, although the only puppet with two strings, was one of the most difficult to operate. In capable hands it slithered, writhed, and struck at the group of children clustered by the stage, sending them scattering and tumbling among the musicians. Three out of the four ministers were said to be the easiest to manipulate as their movements consisted only of nodding their heads wisely and holding their hands up to the king in supplication. The fourth, who played the villain, had to be capable of using either a sword or a stick on a hapless victim, which invariably brought shouts of anger from the audience.

During the third year an apprentice was allowed to work the prized characters in the form of the Ahpyodaw, Mintha, Minthamee, and Zawgyi. The popularity of the Ahpyodaw depended entirely on the personality of the manipulator. One who was of a serious disposition merely went through the correct motions. Another, blessed with an impish exuberance, brought cries of delight and praise. The same applied to the Minthamee. It goes without saying that when a manipulator and a vocalist were well matched, the success of a troupe was assured.

The manipulator could not see the vocalist who sometimes sat behind him, but nevertheless had to match every subtle movement to the vocalist's dialogue or song. Some puppets, like the supernatural beings, were not allowed to touch the floor and had to be held suspended above it—a considerable strain. In some rare instances, a temperamental and exhausted manipulator, irritated beyond endurance by a lengthy recitation from a pompous vocalist, has been known to drop his puppet and walk off the stage. This was guaranteed to bring loud laughter from the equally bored but good-natured audience.

Many manipulators owned their puppets and were responsible for their appearance, lavishing expensive accessories and using good quality materials for the costumes. At home a puppet was known by a nickname and often referred to as the breadwinner. Some treated the little figures as if they were alive and spoke to them. This is not surprising as to the average Burmese the worlds of the natural and the supernatural sometimes overlap and it was accepted that a marionette was imbued with a life of its own. During a performance the vocalist, manipulator, and puppet were believed to merge, all three possessed by the Lamaing Shin Ma *nat*.

5

The Puppet Stage

WHILE one author claimed that fifteenth-century puppet troupes manipulated their figures from tree-tops, others, like the writer Par Nauk, have said that a small triangular *sin* (stage) shaped like the driver's seat of a cart was used (1974).[1] This consisted of seven bamboo poles, each called a *pin* (tree). As no detailed description exists, one must assume that there were four poles in front, two behind, and one at the back, all held together with smaller poles. The structure was completed with a flooring of split bamboo.

The author U Thein Naing believed that prior to the appointment of the first Thabin Wun in 1776, emphasis would have been on dancing, with very few plays performed, but with the subsequent increase in the number of puppets at court in that year, the upgrading of the art began (1966). The Thabin Wun retained the triangular shape of the stage but lengthened the performing area to accommodate the plays that were now being presented. A larger stage, too, was probably more in keeping with the dignity of the court.

U Thaw Zin, in his article on marionettes, described the stage from this period as having seven poles in front, with six gaps in between (1976). It was appropriately called *chauk-khan-sin* (stage with six gaps). The distance between each pole was set at 3 feet, making a total width of 18 feet. At the back there were three posts on each side, leaving four gaps on the left and the right. In time, sections of the stage were given fanciful names, one of these being *galon-taung* (garuda's wings) for the two ends at the front. By 1855 the distance between each pole had increased to 5 feet. This is borne out by Henry Yule who

[1]The association with a cart suggests that some puppet shows, like the *Nebhatkhin* (religious plays) of the fifteenth century, were originally held on the back of one.'

recorded that the stage was now 30 feet wide (1858). Flowers, placed with the offerings on the stage, could only be from species which did not close at night.

A stage was usually erected in the street. Apart from an area set aside for family and friends, the rest of the space was available to anyone, although a central aisle leading to the front of the stage and called a *min-lan* (king's path) had to be kept clear.

Until the late 1880s in Upper Burma, it was mandatory for a marionette stage to be built of bamboo. The long poles in front were stuck into the ground upside down; that is, with the thick end uppermost. When extra lengths were required, a smaller piece was inserted into the cavity of the larger, as it was forbidden to tie the two together. The stage also had to be built facing into the wind (some accounts claim that it had to have its side to the wind). If the show took place in a rice field, the platform was not allowed to straddle the raised boundary path as this would anger the guardian spirit of the field; it, however, did not object to the obstruction being levelled. There is no doubt that observance of all these quaint rules and others too long to list, must have caused untold problems for the troupe.

The stage was built on two levels, with the front lower strip wide enough to roll an unhusked coconut across (about 3 feet) and backed by a white *let-yan* (backdrop) which hung from the *yin-tar* (rail) (see Colour Plate 9). The strings of the puppets merged against this, and also concealed the manipulators up to their waist. Strips of matting were hung from the top front of the stage. These panels were replaced, in about 1910, by a banner decorated with the name of the troupe.

Behind the backdrop the platform was built with a tilt towards the stage, which was flanked by two mat panels on which the puppets were arranged. The first Thabin Wun was probably responsible for designating the correct side for each character. Thus, the area was divided into *let-wair* (left) and *let-yar* (right). (In the 1950s the Dagon Saya Lin Troupe was still following this tradition.) On the left were hung the two demons, alchemist, *naga*, *garuda*, monkey, tiger, parrot, spirit medium, maid of honour, Mintha, Minthamee, an old couple, and Brahmin, together with cymbals, and round and triangular gongs. On the right were hung a *nat* spirit, the horse, two elephants, the king, two senior princes, a hermit, a page boy, and four ministers.

Below the puppets were stored the props. These were holders into which *tha-byai* (*Eugenia grandis*) leaves were inserted to represent the forest and a model of the *nandaw* (palace, complete with three spires and a throne, made of gilded wood and decorated with glass mosaic). There was no scenery. Music and dialogue described the setting, and the imagination of the audience conjured up the rest. Later, additional props were the couch of state, monastery, pagoda, boat, and flying chariot. The first three, being symbols connected with royalty and religion, could not be brought out from under the backdrop, but had to be lowered from the hand-rail. When the show ended, apart from the palace prop, all others were removed first. This important item was then taken down and placed in the leading vehicle; it was forbidden for those following to overtake it. Being the symbol of the Golden Palace (king's authority), this tradition was no longer observed on the demise of the monarchy.

The authors Par Nauk (1974) and Zeya (1964) both claim that during the latter half of the nineteenth century, a central opening in the backdrop, also called a *min-pauk* (royal doorway), was introduced, and that the bamboo poles which help up the two strips of white cloth had to be placed with their tips touching in the middle. However, they do not explain just how the marionettes were produced past this barrier.

An illustration which appeared in *The Graphic* in September 1881 (see Plate 12) shows that the backdrop had been replaced by a sequinned *kalaga* (appliqué hanging) decorated with scenes from popular plays. The troupes in their eagerness to draw the public failed to realize that these ornate cloths competed with the puppets, but the trend continued into the 1920s, when the *kalaga* was replaced by painted scenery. By 1881 the upright bamboo poles at the front of the stage had also given way to wooden posts. These innovations originated in British Burma where the profession had been free, since 1852, from the restrictions imposed by the Thabin Wun. There, brash itinerant troupes were already imitating the style of the court puppet theatre at Mandalay, with some displaying emblems of rank to which they had no right—an unheard of precedent and a punishable offence at the royal capital.

It was during the reign of Mindon (r. 1853–85), whose court was in Mandalay from 1857, that the art of the puppet stage reached new heights of refinement, the vocalists being specially favoured. Puppet companies were graded into six groups by the Thabin Wun after consultations with the king. Each was to be recognized by emblems—or the lack of them—in front of the stage. However, all troupes who performed within the capital were allowed the privilege of flying white pennants.

Although Mindon was not fond of the theatre, he could appreciate a good voice, hence the popularity of the puppet vocalists during his reign. As patron of the arts he would visit the royal theatre when live shows were being performed, though he rarely stayed for long. He decreed that all shows should begin at six in the evening and end at nine. During the reign of his son Theebaw (r. 1878–85), these reverted to the traditional all-night performances. Indeed, by 1882, the demand for theatricals was so great that an extension to the royal theatre was built. Here the court was diverted by famous troupes, and, despite the language barrier, by touring companies from France and India. As soon as one of these foreign shows ended, a stage on wheels would be pushed in front of the audience and a traditional all-night marionette play would begin. In the royal gardens there was another stage designed for puppet shows, but it was only used on informal occasions. These were the golden days for the theatrical profession as both Theebaw and his consort, confined to their palace by political ineptitude, constantly felt the need to be entertained.

Emblems of Rank

The emblems of rank distinguishing the six grades of puppet troupe were as follows:

Thaing: A wand of red lacquer, which was partly or entirely gilded. The tip was bent down with a string, at the end of which was tied a white scarf called a *bwair phyu*. The number of wands awarded ranged from two to five, and these were fastened individually to a front post of the stage. Their presence indicated that the leader of the troupe was entitled to thrash and eject any unwelcome visitors, including drunken members of the royal family or officials, who wandered on to the stage. It is doubtful, however, if this privilege was ever exercised for those in power were capable of exacting a terrible revenge on the socially inferior puppeteers and were thus much feared.

Yaza-mat: Two panels of latticed bamboo painted white fixed on each side of the stage, and sometimes decorated with banana trees in fruit, an auspicious symbol.

Kyar-yat: A long white strip of lace-like cloth, with serrated edges, strung on to a panel of bamboo matting placed in front and above the stage. The numbers ranged from one to three.

At the apex of the marionette profession was the *maha-sin-daw-gyi* (great royal stage), meaning the state troupe, which performed at the *Pwe-kyi-saung* (royal theatre) (Colour Plate 8). This was a gilded pavilion which looked on to the area below where the court sat on carpets arranged in a semicircle. A live performance took place on the ground, and a puppet show on a platform decorated with five gilded *thaing*, three rows of *kyar-yat*, two *yaza-mat*, and banana trees. Part of each front pole, from the stage upwards, was wrapped in white muslin (see Colour Plate 8). The plays enacted were based on the ten final lives of the Buddha and other stories.

Personnel belonging to the *maha-sin-daw-gyi* had certain restrictions placed on them. For instance, a manipulator was forbidden to lift a puppet with his foot to aid its movements, as he did elsewhere.[2] Although the puppeteers were free to perform at religious and secular festivals, they could not take part in cremation ceremonies of eminent monks, which were accompanied by entertainments of all kinds. Members of the court troupe were allocated their own quarter called *Yoke-thay win* (Compound of the Marionettes) at Mandalay.

The second grade of puppet group was the *sin-daw-lat* (royal middle stage), whose emblems of rank consisted of two strips of *kyar-yat*, two *yaza-mat*, and four glided *thaing*. This group was under the patronage of the four Senior Queens and the Crown Prince. When Kanaung Min, the last heir apparent, was assassinated in 1866, it is likely that the company was absorbed into the *maha-sin-daw-gyi*, referred to above.

The *tha-mee-daw-mya-sin* (puppet theatre of the princesses) was the third grade of puppet group. Its emblems were one *kyar-yat*, two *yaza-mat*, and three gilded *thaing*. It was used at functions given by the older princesses, but only with the king's consent. It terminated with the death of Mindon in 1878.

The *sin-daw-galay* (junior royal stage), the troupe whose plays were selected with the royal children in mind, was the fourth group. Although it performed in the royal theatre, it was only allowed to display one *kyar-yat*, two *yaza-mat*, and three gilded *thaing*. It could also offer its services to princes and senior government officials.

Fifthly was the *win-sin* (compound stage), meaning a troupe which entertained the official classes in their large residential compounds. It was allowed one *kyar-yat* as an emblem of its rank. An undated and anonymous *parabaik*[3] (folded paper book) in the Victoria and Albert Museum shows the number of poles on a stage at court had increased to ten. The white flags, trellis

---

[2]To the Burmese this part of the human anatomy is considered 'unclean', and it was therefore a treasonable offence to point it in the direction of the august presence.

[3]The author has discovered that many of the paintings had been copied from a volume by the court artist Kyar Nyunt, dated 1869, which is now in the Musée Guimet, Paris.

partitions, and one *kyar-yat* identifies it as a *win-sin* (Colour Plate 9).

The lowest level of puppet group was the *ah-yat-sin* or itinerant troupe (Colour Plate 10). Although these troupes came under the jurisdiction of the Thabin Wun's department, they were not recognized by the court. Nor were they allowed any emblems on stage, or to enact plays from the ten final lives of the Buddha. Only some of the lesser known *Jataka Tales* and other stories were permissible.

Such rigid classification could not have been upheld for long, and was probably enforced only during the reign of Mindon. After the fall of the dynasty in 1885, the various grades mixed freely, and for about a decade co-operated in trying to preserve the traditions of their art. Financial pressures, however, caused the disintegration of these finer feelings.

Lighting

The idea of an all-night performance originated in the security of a well-guarded town or city. Entertainments were few, and people would have travelled in from the countryside. Rather than leave during the small hours of the morning, it was sensible to spend the night in the company of others.

Tradition required that the person who hired the troupe should provide illumination for the stage. This would have consisted of earthenware bowls with wicks, filled either with crude oil or oil pressed from the seeds of the *ka-lwa* tree (*Cerbera odallam*). In rural areas, long sticks of compressed woodchips mixed with the flammable resin of the *kan-yin* (*Dipterocarpus*) were common. The thick smoke produced by these must have been trying for the puppeteers, who stood bent over the screen. Even at court, where candles and lanterns were used, it must still have been a strain to focus on the small figures. During the second half of the nineteenth century, although 'modern' methods of illumination were being employed, the *sin-daw-galay* usually entertained the royal children mid-morning or late afternoon. The picture which appeared in *The Graphic* (Plate 12) shows a pair of Victorian oil lamps attached to each side of a pole, with a smaller lamp in between. No attempt was made to direct the light on to the marionettes.

The Orchestra (Saing)

The *saing-thamar* (musicians) who accompanied a puppet troupe during the early period of this art's history, probably played a *bon* (drum), *lin-gwin* (cymbals), and a *wa-let-khok* (bamboo clappers). By the eighteenth century the variety of instruments had increased, due partly to the introduction of some new ones from neighbouring cultures (Plate 12), and comprised the following:

1. *Pat-waing* (double-headed drums, graduating in size and held within a circular wooden frame). Originally six in number, these later increased to eight, twelve, and finally sixteen, although twenty-two drums are not unknown.

2. *Kyi-waing* (brass gongs graduating in size, held within a circular frame).

3. *Moung* (large circular gong).

4. *Kyi-see* (triangle gong).

5. *Hnair-gyi* (large oboe).

6. *Hnair-galay* (small oboe).

7. *Chauk-lon-pat* (bass drum).

8. *Pat-ma-gyi* (large double-headed drum hung from a carved pole.)

9. *Sa-khun* (double-headed drum).

10. *Than-lwin* (metallic bells).

Musicians from a *win-sin* or *ah-yat-sin* could only use plain instruments, the one concession being that some of the frames were permitted to be oiled to preserve the wood.

At court, music for important ceremonial events was provided by members of the *saing-daw-gyi* (great royal orchestra) or the state orchestra, composed of the most gifted musicians in the land. At other times its place was taken by the Orchestras of the Royal Left and the Royal Right. The instruments of all

12. *Saing* (orchestra) of a puppet troupe. *Left to right:* bamboo clappers, large drum, oboe, circular wooden frame with drums.

three groups were distinguished by gilding and glass mosaic, and during the short reign of Theebaw, by gilded *thaing* (wands). Gongs, flutes, and oboes were of silver and had to be stored in the royal treasury when not in use. A lithograph in the *Illustrated London News* in 1886 (Plate 13) depicts the last performance given by the court dancers at Mandalay. In the background can be seen the state orchestra displaying six *thaing*.

Some of the senior queens had their own group of musicians, but as they were employed in the women's quarters of the palace, were all female. It would appear that the state orchestra, which was composed of men, was sometimes replaced by these musical ladies, as Albert Fytche, who headed a mission to Mandalay in 1867, discovered when he was invited by Mindon to the royal theatre (1878).

After the fall of the monarchy in Upper Burma it was noticed that puppet companies who had never performed at court began displaying gilded *thaing* in front of their stage, much to the irritation of former members of the *maha-sin-daw-gyi*, who promptly removed theirs.

According to official records of the Mandalay period (1857–85), musicians were originally given crown paddy lands but a salary was later introduced during the reign of Mindon. The collective salary paid to the 133 employed at court was 770 kyats per month, yet on gala occasions among the prizes awarded to outstanding musicians and performers were sumptuous *pasoe* (sarongs) and up to 2,000 silver *daung-dinga* coins. Talent was recognized and the gifted musician vested with minor titles, which also included the revenue of villages. However, these honours were valid only during the lifetime of a king and had to be 'returned' to his successor.

On the evening of a show (about 6 p.m.) given by an *ah-yat-sin*, musicians began playing the cymbals and the large double-headed drum to alert people that a performance was about to begin. At 7 p.m. the whole orchestra played excerpts from their repertoire. The actual show began about 30 minutes later. Each puppet had its individual tune. A character often spoke to

13. The last performance of the state orchestra within the palace of Mandalay in February 1886. The orchestra displays six

the leader of the musicians—this was called *saing-sint*—addressing him as 'lord of the orchestra' and either coaxed or demanded that an appropriate tune be provided for whatever event was at hand: a battle, the crossing of a river, flying through the air, or entering a dark forest:

'Now thunder forth a bold inspiring strain
Whose echoes, spreading far and wide, shall
shake the earth to its foundations.'[4]

[4]An extract from the play *Ngwe-taung* (Silver Hill), which dominated the marionette stage and live theatre until well into this century. It was one of the first Burmese plays to be translated into English, by Lieutenant Sladen and Colonel Sparks in 1856.

6

A Puppet Performance

THE first half of a performance in the early 1900s began with a musical interlude symbolizing the multiple destructions and re-creations of the world. This was followed by the introduction of a series of characters dancing in a magical forest glade somewhere in the *Himawunta* (Himalayas). As this sequence was designed with children in mind, it included animals and fantastic creatures. Towards midnight, after the obligatory royal audience and the appearance of the Mintha and Minthamee, the second part, which consisted of the play proper, commenced.

The Introductory Himawunta Sequence

The Burmese believe that the world was destroyed sixty-four times by the three elements of *mee* (fire), *lay* (wind), and *yae* (water). The burning of the earth began with the appearance of seven suns and is said to have occurred fifty-six times. Strong winds then wrought destruction once. Torrential rains, in turn, devastated the earth seven times, during which time waves and water spouts assumed such gigantic proportions that the highest level of the spirit world of the Brahma was inundated. Life is said to have appeared after each annihilation, only to be destroyed.

However, it is not clear just how or who it was that survived all these apocalyptic horrors and lived to tell the tale in a work called the *Adikappa Kyam*. A clue may lie in a comment made by Hla Thamein, who said that it was written by ancient rishis after meditation, and later absorbed into the *Pitaka* (Buddhist Canon) (1968). The authors were undoubtedly Indian, as many of the beliefs in Burma originated from that country.

These cataclysmic events were announced from backstage by

the clashing of the cymbals seven times. The gong was then struck once, followed by a rapid rhythm on the drums, the sound symbolizing the impact of the huge raindrops on the swirling waters. This sequence was repeated three times by each instrument to represent the destructiveness of the elements.

The first marionette to appear was the Natkadaw (spirit medium). It danced and propitiated the unseen forces of the district, town, or village in which the show was being held, a ritual regarded as essential in order to purify the area of all malevolent influences.

An ode to Thagyar Min (Indra) was then sung by the vocalist for the Mintha. It described the worlds of spirits, and how the four great islands and the two thousand lesser ones' had been created once the churning waters had subsided. In the centre was Mount Meru, ringed by mountains and the forests of the *Himawunta*. Around these were the seven great lakes, the five great rivers, the five hundred smaller rivers, and the four great oceans. In the heavens had been created the sun, moon, and stars.

Other ritual songs to the thirty-seven national *nat* and the local *nat* were sung by the vocalist for the Minthamee. This was an important moment in the show, and the vocal talents of the two leading singers were critically noted by the audience. Members of the orchestra, too, showed off their skill with their chosen instrument.

The spirit medium was replaced by the Ahpyodaw (see Colour Plate 1) on the second and third night. Her routine once included the distinctive movements of twelve characters mentioned earlier which have remained consistent in the ever-changing set of puppets.[1]

A horse called Ajaneya, which had the ability to fly, followed the Ahpyodaw. It symbolized the *Ahthawani* (*Asavani*) *netkhat*, a constellation which appeared at the creation of the world. The figure is borrowed from Hindu mythology and represents

[1]Before the commencement of a live show, a similar sequence, known as the Dance of the Ahpyodaw, is performed by a senior member from among the female dancers.

the Ashwins, physicians to the gods, who accompany Surya the sun.

Ajaneya was brought out facing the audience. It sees the vast expanse of the earth and is tempted down and performs four dances to a tune called the *myin-tet-yodaya* (music for a horse in the Ayutthaya style), its anklets of small bells jingling merrily. Those who were knowledgeable about puppet-lore knew that if the horse appeared from the top left of the screen, the palace prop would later be placed on the right, and that only one kingdom would feature in the play. If the horse entered from the central opening, which was a feature in some troupes, the existence of two kingdoms on the left and right would be noted. The sequence ended with the horse, which was manipulated by eleven strings, galloping off over the backdrop.

On the departure of this animal, a monkey, the first earth-bound creature to be created, was brought out (Colour Plate 11). It too danced then ended its act by swinging off the stage.

A tiger, attracted by the commotion, now appeared and postured, opening its huge jaws in time to the music, chasing its tail, and rushing at the children standing near the stage. It was the only puppet which required two manipulators.

In some troupes the animal either appeared on its own or in a playlet, the favourite involving two of the thirty-seven *nat* known as the Shwephyin brothers. The play centred on Ma Mai U, a married woman who attracts the attention of the younger brother, but repulses his advances. In fury, he orders his tiger to attack her. Although the story was well known, the audience would watch with consternation as Ma Mai U, who sat weaving, was stalked, grabbed, and worried by the beast (see Colour Plate 20). It eventually killed her and she, too, became a *nat*. On the night this episode was included, offerings were placed before the puppets of the two spirits and the tiger. The three puppets were also hung separately from the rest.

Another playlet which involved the tiger used the elderly couple, whose dialogue could become quite bawdy. After many ribald comments which the audience found highly amusing, the sketch ended with the irritable old lady going behind the bushes to relieve herself, unaware that the tiger was watching her. This scene caused much agitation among the audience, who yelled out warnings, but the tiger always exited with his victim, who continued to scold as she was carried off.

Sometimes the tiger entered from one entrance and the black elephant (Plate 14) from the other. After they had danced they

14. Sin-net (black elephant). Early twentieth century. (Courtesy of the Powell-Cotton Museum)

became belligerent and a fight ensued, with voices from backstage shouting encouragement. The white elephant was rarely used, and then it was only ridden by the king or prince.

On the departure of the tiger and the elephant, two demons armed with weapons—either a long staff or, more unusually, two short swords or sticks—appeared and performed a martial dance, swaggering about and threatening the crowd (Colour Plates 12 and 13 and Plate 15). Both their costumes are usually green in colour and probably symbolized the dark forest which is their habitat. After skirmishing, the music quickened to a faster beat known as *karaung*, and the dance ended with the two locked in combat. Some troupes introduced the demons immediately after the monkey, whom they chased off the stage.

A Zawgyi, skilled in the art of alchemy and flight, slowly descended from the sky (Colour Plate 14 and Plate 16). Dressed in a red robe and clutching a wand, he sang about the beauty of the forest while searching for magic herbs which he ground into a potion. After swallowing the draught, he danced. As the movements were complicated, only a master puppeteer could handle this figure. Indeed, the skill with which the Zawgyi was manipulated was carefully observed by the audience, especially when he was made to walk up and down twirling his wand. Unlike some of the other characters, the Zawgyi's costume does not reach the ground, preventing the manipulator from surreptitiously moving the bottom half of the puppet with his foot. To overcome this difficulty, tiny lead weights were attached to the heels. When the string to each foot was lifted and subsequently released, it looked as if the figure was walking. When it balanced on one end of the wand, the manipulator stuck his foot out from under the curtain and gripped the base with his toes, while the marionette above performed acrobatic tricks.

Troupes from about the 1920s introduced a second Zawgyi so that the pair could show off their prowess. One was known as the Nan Zaw (palace Zawgyi), a refined and splendidly dressed personage, while the other was the rustic or Taw Zaw, a comic figure. At the end of the sequence, the manipulator would wind all the strings around the puppet, and in a twisting

15. Belu (demon) with clubs. Late nineteenth century. (Courtesy of the Pitt Rivers Museum)

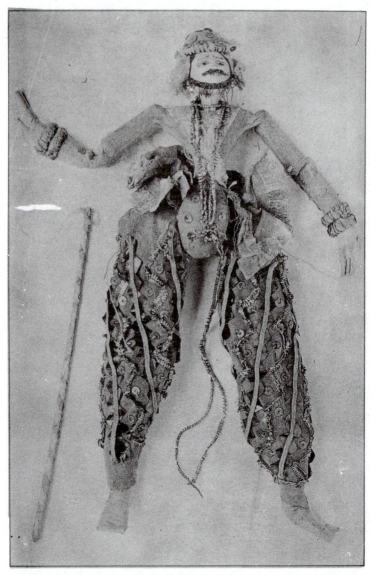

16. **Zawgyi** (alchemist) with wand. Late nineteenth century. (Courtesy of the **Pitt** Rivers Museum)

motion send it whirling through the air before finally leaping over the backdrop.

During the entire *Himawunta* sequence, the characters followed one another in rapid succession. A gap was never allowed to occur as the puppeteers knew that this would break the concentration of their audience. Traditionally, there was an interval following the dance of the Zawgyi, which allowed members of the orchestra time to rest, as they had been performing since early evening. These scenes from the *Himawunta* forests were repeated during the succeeding two nights; only the main plays changed.

The Second Part of a Performance

Part Two always began within the palace with four ministers appearing in order of seniority. The figures were brought out with their arms swinging in an exaggerated manner.

The four identified themselves as ministers of the kingdom which appeared in the play; this part was known as the *taing-pye-tair-gan* (establishing the kingdom). Discussions then took place on the finer points of religious and secular texts, and on the affairs of government. After they had retired, a page boy, called the Thu-nge-daw (Colour Plate 15), was produced. He danced and prepared for the arrival of the king. This puppet was made slightly smaller than the others, and was usually manipulated by the trainee for the Mintha. In some troupes this was the moment when the model of the palace was lowered on to the stage.

Royal music sounded, and the king appeared with his ministers (Plate 18). This was a very formal moment and elaborate court language was used. The Mintha, Minthamee, and their clown attendants then made a grand entrance. At the end of the ritualized conversation between the pair and the king, the audience ended, and the royal figure and his ministers were removed. The two principal characters, both dressed in brilliant costumes, then proceeded to sing and dance in a musical interlude called the *thit-sar-htar* (swearing eternal love). This usually lasted for about two hours, when a short interval

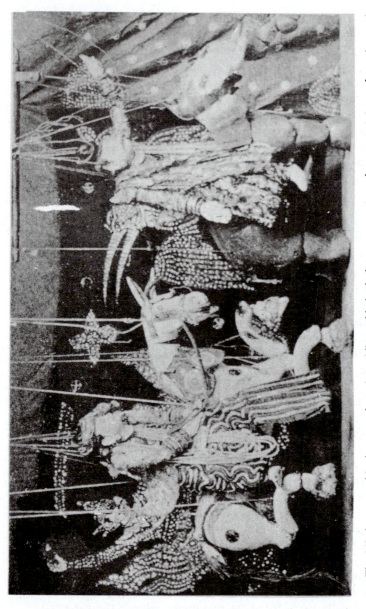

17. The Mintha on a white horse, and a prince riding a black elephant journey through a magical forest. Late nineteenth century. From Max and Bertha Ferrars, *Burma*, 1900.

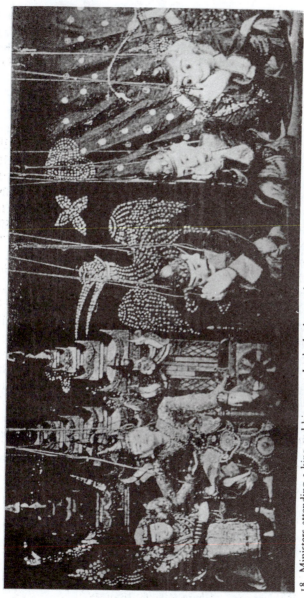

18. Ministers attending a king and his queen. In the background can be seen the symbol of the palace and sequinned *kalaga* which replaced the traditional white cloth. Late nineteenth century. From Max and Bertha Ferrars, *Burma*, 1900.

followed and the play proper began. Sometimes a change of costume was made, but in most troupes the Mintha and Minthamee slipped into their new roles, still dressed in their sumptuous robes.

The Repertoire of Plays

Some Buddhist sects are said to have frowned upon entertainments of any kind. As a result, plays performed by early puppet and live troupes were probably derived from the better known *Jataka Tales*. Propaganda, doubtless spread by the performers, claimed that watching these religious plays brought merit. Later, playlets based on a selection from local history and folk-lore were added though the emphasis was on religion in order to gain the approval of the clergy.

In 1733 the first full-length play, *Maniket*, was produced by Padaythayaza (1684–1752), a poet and minister of the last two kings of the Nyaungyan Dynasty (1599–1752). Being a popular play, the Thabin Wun's puppeteers would undoubtedly have included it in their repertoire. Another, which originated at Shwebo and was named after the heroine *Mai-zar-yu*, was set during the days of the Burma–Thai Wars of 1760–7. However, these two plays do not appear to have survived into the 1820s as they are not included in the official list of puppet plays performed at court.

It was also from this period that ten of the *Jataka Tales*, known as the *Zat-gyi-sair-bwe* (ten great *Jataka*), became increasingly popular. Each symbolized a particular virtue:

1. *Tay-mi zat* (*Temyia*) relinquishment.
2. *Za-na-ka zat* (*Mahajanaka*) fearlessness.
3. *Thu-wun-na-shan* (*Sama*) benevolence.
4. *Nay-mee zat* (*Nimi*) determination.
5. *Ma-haw-tha-da zat* (*Mahosadha*) sagacity.
6. *Bu-ye-dat zat* (*Bhuridatta*) tenacity.
7. *San-da-gon-mar zat* (*Canda Kumara*) patience.
8. *Na-ya-da zat* (*Narada*) imperturbability.
9. *We-dura zat* (*Vidhura Pandita*) honesty.
10. *Way-than-daya zat* (*Vessantara*) generosity.

By the second half of the nineteenth century, all the plays had been neatly categorized and came under the heading of:

1. *Nibatwin Mahawin zat* (plays based on religious texts, such as the *Jataka Tales*).

2. *Phaya-thamaing* (plays based on the history of a pagoda). There are many thousands of stupas in the country, each with its tale of myth, magic, and historical episodes.

3. *Yazawin zat* (factual or semi-fictional plays based on the lives of historical characters).

4. *Dandaye* (folk-tales).

5. *Hto Zat* (fictional plays).

A troupe with a strong feminine lead would naturally choose a play in which the heroine featured prominently. Other stories featured an animal. If the company did not possess the right figure, either one of the principal puppets, wearing an appropriate mask, would assume the role. The mask was perched on top of the head and never covered the face (Plate 19).

In 1871 Mindon convened the Fifth Great Buddhist Synod with the aim of establishing Mandalay as the religious and cultural centre of Burma. As a result, the 1870s saw an increase in plays based on Buddhist stories. At the Myin-mo-pwe festival, held in mid-October, Setkya-devi, Mindon's Chief Queen, is said to have hired troupes to perform religious plays at the hundred or so monasteries in the capital. During the day, live actors entertained, and at night their places were taken by the puppeteers.

Dramatists were adept at holding the audience's attention, one of their ploys being to emphasize the great suffering experienced by the Mintha and Minthamee, both of whom, to a European observer, would have masochistic tendencies. The brave hero, who could vanquish demons and other supernatural enemies, invariably became submissive and grovelling in the hands of authority—a subtle form of intimidation and a reminder from the all-powerful crown to the audience.[2] Nevertheless, stories had to have a suitably happy ending. Virtue was

---

[2] Many young modern males, watching an old play, find this behaviour objectionable and cannot understand why the hero is not aggressive. They see it as a slur on Burmese masculinity.

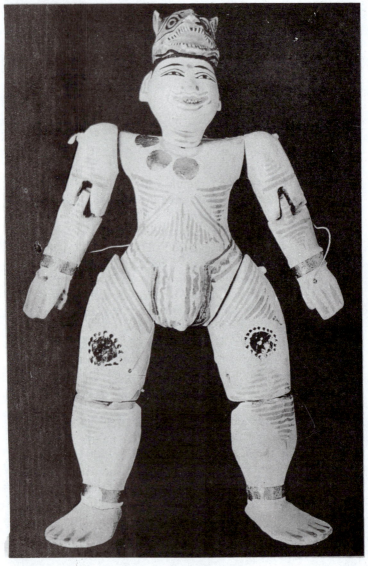

19. Boy puppet with a tiger mask perched on top of his head. *c.*1880.
(Courtesy of the Pitt Rivers Museum)

rewarded and evil punished. Plays in which a character died were frowned upon, and the person who hired the troupe was entitled to refuse to pay the troupe. If the scenario required the death of the two principals, they subsequently had to be brought back to life by the gods. None the less, there were plays based on the impermanence of life. These were performed at funerals where the bereaved family had to provide entertainment for visitors during the wake.

According to a list compiled by the Wetmasut Mingyi, a minister of Mindon, and later Theebaw, over a hundred plays were used by the court marionette troupes. Although the list is not complete—as equally famous titles are known to have been omitted—the large number indicates the preference of the ruling classes for this form of entertainment.

Plays written for the court continued to be performed for a few decades after the fall of the dynasty, but many did not survive the decline of the puppet stage. Moreover, new plays for the live theatre, which were printed in British Burma from about 1872, gained in popularity. According to the writer Hmawbee Saya Thein, by the first two decades of this century over 500 titles had been circulated, of which 125 have survived in the British Library in London (c.1930). Some of the more popular were adapted by a different class of puppeteer, one with modern ideas and desperate for bookings.

It was once the tradition for the person who wished to hire a troupe and see a particular play enacted to make his request to the proprietor with a bowl of fruit and flowers. If a preference for a particular play was not indicated, the leader would discuss with his colleagues the historical and mythical background of the area they were travelling to and choose an appropriate one. With the rise in the huge number of plays, featuring a diversity of ethnic characters, troupes touring among the Arakanese, Shan, Karen, or Mon communities would select plays in which the national heroes of these groups predominated.

7

The Spread and Decline of
the Puppet Theatre

THE British, although unpopular, did provide a stable government after they annexed Lower Burma. This resulted in a growing Burmese merchant and official class. In 1877 the opening of the Rangoon–Prome railway encouraged marionette companies from the independent kingdom of Upper Burma to travel down to the prosperous Delta areas.

Troupes from British Burma also travelled to Mandalay where they were referred to by traditionalists as *auk-ah-yat-sin* (puppeteers from the lower country), a denigrating term which implied that they were lacking in experience. Nevertheless, they were popular with the majority of their audiences, who probably found their freer attitudes novel and refreshing. These touring companies also tried their best to gain admittance to the Golden Palace so that their prestige would be enhanced. Many succeeded, and on their return proudly displayed whatever gifts Theebaw and Suphayarlat had bestowed on them, and related their experiences from the stage. Some leading vocalists and manipulators, overcome with nationalistic fervour, called themselves *pyi-daw-pyan* (one who had returned from the royal country).

In April 1880 *The Graphic*, at the height of the puppet theatre's popularity, devoted a centre spread to a marionette performance at Rangoon.

The chief incident of the festival is a puppet pooay, or play, performed at night. The whole scene resembles a vast picnic, and thousands of people, with carts laden with refreshments, begin to arrive on the spot early in the evening and to encamp round the puppet stage. The carts and oxen are so placed as to form a large ring, and the enclosed space is left for the accommodation of the spectators. At seven the puppet performance begins, lasting until five in the morning.

Another illustration, which included the orchestra used by a puppet troupe (see Plate 12), followed in September 1881:

This is an entertainment of which the Burmese, both men and women, are passionately fond. They will often sit from 8 p.m. till 2 to 3 a.m. on the following morning, listening to one of these plays. The dolls are cleverly worked with strings and judging from the hearty laughter of the audiences, the dialogue of the puppets must be excessively witty if not highly refined.

George Scott (Shway Yoe), who attended a performance by the ex-Thabin Wun, U Thar Pyaw, said that the moment the singer's voice was heard 'there is not a sound, the whole great crowd, and it must not be forgotten that the performance is in the open air, is hushed to its farthest limits, and not until the passage is finished does the usual buzz and chatter begin again' (1896).[1]

After the Third Anglo-Burmese War of 1885, there was a general exodus of craftsmen and entertainers from the north to the greener pastures of the south. For those who felt incapable of uprooting themselves, the annexation was undoubtedly traumatic. Puppeteers who clung to the old traditions and refused to accept change fell by the wayside. Others, among them the vocalists who had performed at court, joined theatrical companies and became known as *sin-daw-kya* (he who fell from the royal stage), where they were welcomed and respected for their expertise. The situation resulted in a shortage of apprentices willing to undertake the arduous training in puppetry and to accept its poor rewards.

Understandably, with such a high concentration of artistes in Lower Burma, competition within the entertainment world became intense. Some troupes gave free performances just to announce their presence. The more astute among the puppeteers exploited every opportunity to extend their popularity—a trait first seen in the Tavoy area of Tenasserim. There, the ancient sport of buffalo fighting, which had been revived from about

[1]The privilege of hiring U Thar Pyaw for two nights was said to have been 450 rupees, a substantial sum of money in those days.

1850, was attracting huge crowds by 1878. The craze, which lasted nearly thirty years, had to be stopped, however, because of its effect on gambling and crime. The ban did not please the local inhabitants who considered it a traditional sport. As a result, puppet troupes began introducing buffalo fights in their shows, an additional sequence which became immensely popular. But this, too, is said to have caused a further outbreak of gambling (the manipulators were probably paid to fix the contests by the organizers). Fights erupted among the audience, and the item had to be lawfully removed from the programme.

By the late 1890s diversification in the use of puppets was beginning to appear. Photographs from the period show puppets and even performances on fantastically shaped bamboo and paper structures made for the cremation ceremonies of monks (Plate 20). This was a previously unheard of event and can only have occurred because of financial problems. (The figures were removed before the torch was applied.)

During the early part of this century, among the many casualties of the puppet theatre was U Phu Nyo (1861–1929), a once famous Minthamee vocalist who was said to have been so overcome with acute depression that he threw his troupe's entire collection of marionettes into the river.

Despite declining bookings from about 1920, a few troupes tried to re-establish themselves with bigger and modern-looking marionettes, but were generally unsuccessful in their attempts. Some of the figures were said to have been about 4 feet high and because of their weight caused some of the manipulators to fall off the stage. Some troupes introduced *yein* (chorus dances) with up to six puppets moving in unison. The 'chorus lines' were composed of either young men, girls, Zawgyi, or exotic mythological beings. Some figures were made to flash electric torches at the audience as they danced; others, influenced by foreign films, were called *bioscope yein*. New ethnic characters, such as Europeans, Chinese, Indians, and some of the tribal figures from the hills, now appeared with the traditional puppets. Despite these innovations, the popularity of the marionette theatre continued to plummet. It was the era of the

20. A bamboo and paper structure made for the cremation ceremony of a monk. Puppets are being worked by a man standing underneath the elephant. *c.* 1890.

ah-nyeint (a variety show composed of young females). Circuses from India, live theatrical performances, films (both native and foreign), and other forms of entertainment all took their toll on the puppet theatre. In Mandalay, which was still considered to be the centre for the arts, only a handful of established companies found continuous work. Others, less fortunate, did not perform at all.

8

Post-war Puppet Troupes

AFTER the depredations of the Japanese Occupation, which finally ended in 1945, Burma, which suffered like many other South-East Asian countries, tried to return to some form of normality. In 1948 it regained its independence from Britain, but in a short time large areas of the country were terrorized by insurgency. Understandably, this effected the travelling entertainment industry.

In the few towns and villages which enjoyed security, members of some puppet troupes, who knew no other form of livelihood, regrouped, but having lost their possessions had to commission new sets of puppets. Others, like Ponnapyan U Kyaw Aye, managed to save their collection and were one of the first to resume giving performances.

Beginning from the 1950s the setting on a puppet stage became a replica of the live theatre. Depending on the whim of the leader of a troupe, a show could begin with a short play and then introduce characters from the *Himawunta* sequence. A puppet resembling Tarzan would sometimes made an appearance accompanied by the monkey. The tiger and elephant, preparing to fight in an enchanted forest glade, would be confronted by a European hunter with a rifle, which was fired with a loud bang. An English lady walking her little dog was quite likely to encounter the *garuda* and *naga*. Playlets which showed characters in modern dress who drove cars, rode motor cycles, and flew in aeroplanes became popular during the first half of the performance and were sandwiched between brief appearances by the traditional puppets.

Dagon Saya Lin, one of the more prominent puppeteers, now began his show with the king of the gods slowly descending from above the curtain-rail, while the Mintha's voice sang the ritual songs to which the Natkadaw would normally have mimed. He also increased the number of horses to four and made many other innovations. In an interview he announced that he had broken with tradition twenty years earlier by appointing a female puppeteer called Awba Tin, although it should be pointed out that a lady by the name of Ma Sein Kha was already performing as a Minthamee vocalist in the late nineteenth century. Other female performers were soon to follow as young men became reluctant to take the role of the Minthamee. Indeed, feminists will nod with approval on learning that after being barred from the 'sacred' stage for centuries, not only did women rightfully play the part of the Minthamee, but some, like Aung Thein and Bala Sein, found fame as vocalists for the male lead!

In 1960 there were only five active marionette troupes in Rangoon: Nyaungdone U Ba Kyaw; Hlaing-maha-thabin-sindaw-ahphwe; Ponnapyan U Kyaw Aye; Pyidawaye-yokeson-ahphwe; and the Shwebo Tin Maung Troupe—the only one to continue enjoying popularity during this bleak period. U Tin Maung, the owner and vocalist for the troupe, had become an acknowledged leader in his profession from the second half of the 1950s, and was to continue so until the early 1970s. Although he changed the style and technique of a perform-ance to suit modern tastes, he retained many of the traditions. Some of his marionettes were acquired from the families of puppeteers who had performed for the *maha-sin-daw-gyi*. He also revived plays from the nineteenth century. When he died in 1976 his daughter (Plate 21), an accomplished manipulator, took over the company.

A performance, witnessed by the author in 1960, was im-pressively lit and the scenes given a dream-like and magical quality by colourful spotlights. Fluorescent paints, which were all the rage at the time in the theatrical profession, were used on some of the costumes and scenery; these, picked out by ultraviolet lights, produced amazing effects.

In 1967 a government publication claimed that puppetry was being taught in the State School of Drama and Music, to which

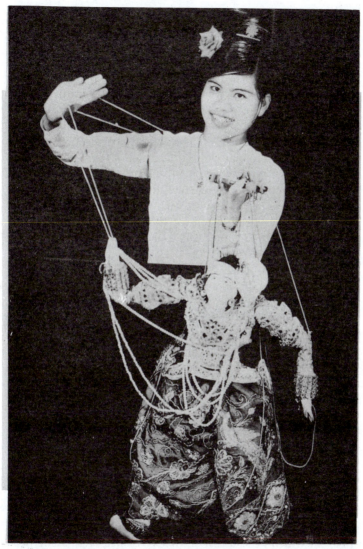

21. Mintha (prince) being manipulated by the daughter of the late Shwebo Tin Maung. *c.* 1977.

leading puppeteers made occasional visits, but this was short-lived. By then, only three out of the five professional troupes of 1960 were still performing in Rangoon.

During the late 1950s the Ministry of Union Culture often presented visiting foreign cultural delegations with sets of rare puppets from the second half of the nineteenth century, many of which had been used at the Mandalay court. Having escaped the destruction of the Japanese Occupation in the early 1940s, it is unfortunate that such valuable objects of theatrical history should end up in foreign collections.

Hla Thamein, writing in 1968, listed twenty-seven companies for the entire country. He claimed that some were booked for about a hundred performances each season (an unusually high number considering the state of the puppet theatre) and the lesser known ones, about fifty. The charge was said to be 400 kyats per night.

According to U Khin Mg Phyu, an official at the National Museum in Rangoon, in 1981 three small troupes were known to exist in Lower Burma: Twante Ko Kywetkalay Yoke-thay; Sein Lin Yaung; and Sein Party Yoke-thay. The others had either sold their puppets or were only performing inter-mittently.

In the late 1960s and early 1970s Burmese puppets began appearing in the antique markets and shops of London. At first they were of the best possible quality, but as the supply of the older pieces ran out, new ones were made and smuggled out of the country into Thailand, and from there to dealers in the West. The figures, a sad echo of the beautifully crafted nineteenth-century pieces, are cleverly aged but cannot compare favourably with some of the superb examples in foreign collections (Colour Plates 16–18). One had the distinct feeling that the art of puppetry was now in its death throes. It was therefore encouraging to read Hla Thamein's article in *Sawaddi* (1986) in which he said that shows were once again being held, albeit at strategic tourist locations. However, recent guide books and articles on Burma carry pictures of rather sad-

looking puppeteers valiantly exhibiting their skills and manipulating garish dolls which in no way resemble the splendid
pieces seen in early photographs. In one, the owner of the only
puppet troupe at Pagan said that the Burmese people had lost
interest and were quite indifferent to the survival of the puppet
theatre. The all-night shows are also now a thing of the past. In
1989 the military government imposed a 11 p.m.–4 a.m.
curfew which continues at the time of writing. As a con-
sequence, a considerable number of theatrical troupes have
been forced to disband.

Photographs of a puppet troupe performing in Rangoon in
1991 show that the Mintha, Minthamee, and a few other
female characters were painted to conform to contemporary
ideas of beauty (Plate 22). Change is inevitable, and although
the quintessentially Burmese face of the Mandalay period has
finally been replaced, it is encouraging to see the tremendous
efforts undertaken by the few remaining puppeteers to prevent
this old art from fading away, and having the puppets relegated
to a museum showcase.

Today's youth find traditional forms of entertainment out-
dated and are more impressed by Western style music and the
ubiquitous video movies. As the majority can barely understand
the stately prose of the old court language, the dialogue in the
few remaining marionette and live theatrical troupes has been
forced to modernize. This was noticed as early as the 1960s by
the writer U Thaw Zin, who in an article roundly condemned
the new breed of puppeteers and playwrights for pandering to
modern audiences. He complained that the dialogue in the
traditional plays had become too colloquial and was wholly
inappropriate to the various periods in which they were set. At
rehearsals, a gauche young Mintha vocalist wanted to know
why he had to wait more than fifteen minutes while the villain
gave a long-winded recital before striking him, when it could
have been over and done with in just five seconds. Purists
among the audience may well wince at the crude utterances of
characters dressed in historically inaccurate costumes; the latter,

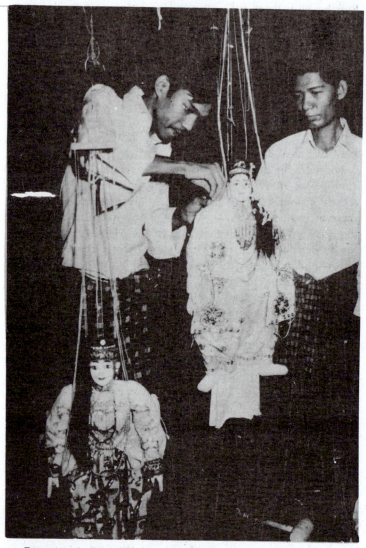

22. Puppeteers in Rangoon, 1991. The puppets' faces have been painted to conform to contemporary ideas of beauty. (Courtesy of Sylvia E. Lu)

for both puppet and the live theatre, are glamorized and flashy versions from the late nineteenth century and are the standard costumes for all period plays.

U Thaw Zin also said that some of the nineteenth-century scripts, which had somehow survived, were still in the possession of the families of ex-puppeteers, and was deeply concerned that they would soon be lost. Fortunately, his article alerted the appropriate authorities and many have been saved for the nation.

Traditionalists and lovers of all that belongs to Old Burma must feel depressed at the changes taking place to the stringed ones. They should, however, take heart that although the *yoke-thay* figures are now a mere parody of their former selves, the real treasures from the puppet theatre are indestructible and will continue to survive in the form of nineteenth- and early twentieth-century plays, the unlocking and competent translation of which should one day allow them to take their rightful place in the world's theatrical heritage.

9

The Influence of Puppets
on Burmese Dance and Crafts

THE *Rajavamsa* (Chronicle of Kings) tells us that in 1591 the Arakanese King Min Phalaung (r. 1571–93) rebuilt the Urittaung Pagoda near his capital Mrauk U on the west coast of Burma, and celebrated its completion by holding a great festival. Along the processional paths the 'representations of the 101 races of men, of scenes in the 550 *Jataka Tales*, of aquatic monsters were paraded'. The author U Min Naing claims in his Burmese language book on dance and drama that many of the figures were of wood and were designed to act out selected episodes from the Ten Lives of the Buddha. Although he does not say how the characters were operated, he does mention that their movements came to be imitated by Arakanese dancers, and as such *yoke-thay-ah-ka* (dance of the puppets) became a national dance for several hundred years.

In Upper Burma, the traditional heartland of the Burmese race, female dancers from the second half of the nineteenth century thought it elegant to mimic the movements of their puppet counterparts. To be told that one danced 'like a stringed doll' was extremely complimentary. An expression, probably coined during this period, proclaimed that 'humans should dance like marionettes and marionettes like humans'.[1] As a result, some of the puppet dances found their way into the repertoire of live dancers. The aggressive posturing of the demon, for instance, and the sprightly Dance of the Ahpyodaw duplicate the movements of these characters. *Yein* choruses, wearing papier mâché horse head-dresses, also imitate this graceful puppet as they strut and gallop around in intricate formations.

[1] This applied only to some forms of dancing and went out of fashion from about the 1930s, but was revived again in the late 1950s.

While the gestures of marionettes have had to change to suit contemporary tastes, conversely many of the original movements have been preserved by live dancers. The traditional duet performed by the Mintha and Minthamee during the second half of the show, for example, is faultlessly mimicked by a human couple, and is a favourite dance item. But to see how an earlier prince, princess, and their clownish attendant entertained their audience, one has to witness a performance of a little-known rural dance in Upper Burma called the *Shwebo-bongyi*. Its stylized and stately movements are believed to have remained unchanged through the centuries, any modifications being discouraged by the elders. Until about 1920 the feminine lead was always played by a young man.

The Zawgyi, a popular puppet character whose dance movements involve spectacular leaps and whirls, is also copied by agile male dancers (Plate 23). Phaunglin village, near Salin in Central Burma, is particularly famous for its group of young men, known as the Phaunglin Zaw Yein, who enjoy a reputation for the strict observance of the original movements, many of which have been altered by modern manipulators outside the village. U Min Naing claims that this 200-year-old dance has been handed down from father to son and that outsiders are discouraged from taking part.

Among the basic movements still taught to trainee dancers are those used by puppets. These gestures are said to be invaluable for acquiring perfect control and for disciplining the body. These *ah-yoke-kyo-ka* can still be seen in special performances staged by the Ministry of Union Culture. The characters listed above, together with others, have become a part of the *zat-pwe* (a combination of variety show and period play), and are in fact a mirror image of those from the marionette stage.

A manipulator, too, borrowed from the live theatre, his only ambition being to make his puppet move with all the grace a human dancer could exhibit. Conscious of changing tastes he strove to delight his audiences with fashionable and current modes of dancing. As a result, it is sometimes difficult to say precisely who was responsible for inventing a particular style.

23. The author performing the Dance of the Zawgyi (alchemist) in 1965.

Aside from its influence on dance, the puppet theatre had an impact on the crafts of the country. Burma was once renowned for its elaborately carved monasteries which often contained panels of popular characters and scenes from the better-known plays of the day. Woodcarvers and sculptors were clearly influenced by marionettes, as the postures of the figures they created are similar to the movements seen on stage. Facial expressions on many examples are invariably rendered in the quizzical marionette style (Plate 24).

Lacquerware is still produced in large quantities at Kyaukkar and at the ancient city of Pagan. The colours, which may appear garish and overpowering compared to the more sophisticated Chinese and Japanese hues, have an exuberant charm of

24. Brass figure of an old man with the expression cast in the quizzical puppet style. *c.* 1910.

their own. Over the years numerous designs have evolved, one of these being the *yoke-thay* or 'small marionette' style (Colour Plate 19). Rare pieces of decorated lacquerware from the 1830s are often incised with pictures of popular characters from the puppet theatre, such as the Mintha, Minthamee, and the Zawgyi. Stories which appealed to audiences were often immortalized on the sides of bowls, with each tableau separated by the symbolic sprig of leaves. Many a play which has now been lost survives only in this form.

Puppeteers also helped to popularize the *kalaga* (applique hangings) which are unique to Burma. Being a tropical country, many of the interiors of palaces and houses were built with few partitions so that cool air could circulate. *Kalaga* were thus used to provide some form of privacy, and were originally made of plain strips of cloth. In a painting conserved in the Victoria and Albert Museum (Colour Plate 9), the example displayed on stage consists of a simple wave pattern. However, by the 1870s its appearance had undergone a dramatic change. With foreign materials readily available, *kalaga* workers began producing memorable moments from successful plays. These were lavishly decorated with sequins and imitation gems. They became so popular they were hung not only in the interior of a reception hall but also on its exterior. It also became fashionable to use one of these brilliant hangings as a pall at elaborate funeral ceremonies of eminent ecclesiastics and laymen. Needless to say, the figures with which a *kalaga* was decorated were depicted in the stylized marionette tradition made up from pieces of rich, colourful materials (Colour Plate 20).

At the height of the puppet craze during the second half of the nineteenth century, much of the stock found in toy stalls comprised puppets (Plate 25). These came in a variety of sizes and designs. Some of the human figures were made of clay, cotton, and paper and were clothed in colourful robes of cloth, tinsel, sequins, and gold paper. In the 1900s the more expensive wooden models were hardly distinguishable from those used on stage, the main difference being that they were produced on a smaller scale. Sadly, none have survived in Burma. To

25. Toy stall selling puppets: From C. A. Gordon, *Our Trip to Burmah*, 1875.

examine these unusual and delightful pieces, one has now to visit some of the museums in Britain, in particular the Pitt Rivers Museum in Oxford which has an unmatched collection (Plates 15 and 16).

Shops selling modern toy puppets can, however, still be found in the covered paths leading to pagodas in Burma. Children still find them fascinating. Girls especially love the Mintha and Minthamee, while boys take to the tiger, the Zawgyi in his bright red robe, and the gleaming white horse with gold trappings. This puppet is still made—in three sizes—at Prome, Rangoon, Sagaing, and Zalun. The largest, which is about 1½ feet high, is richly decorated and is produced exclusively for the *nat* trade. These horses, which have six strings, are hung throughout the country in shrines dedicated to the Myin-phyu-shin (Lord of the White Horse), a twelfth-century equerry to Prince Narapatisithu, later king of Pagan (r. 1174–1211), who had the equerry killed for neglect of duty. This sad tale has become a popular play of the marionette stage.

Puppets have exercised an influence not only on the dance and crafts of the country but also on its literature. Talented nineteenth- and early twentieth-century playwrights, among them celebrated Mintha vocalists, who wrote exclusively for the puppet theatre, were much admired. Their descriptive passages were especially savoured. These are so diverse in style and composition that they have been categorized under numerous headings. Old folk songs, like the *Shwebo-bongyi-than*, often mention a marionette show, thereby helping to throw more light on the early history and presentation of the puppet theatre. Today, a young mother watching her toddler lifting his little feet and stamping sees the movements of a Zawgyi and encourages him to dance by clapping and singing:

Ma ma lay bair pyinna hnin min shar lo chu-ay chauk khan sin paw ka pyo do maung nyo nyo lay zaw ka lo chu-ay.
When you grow up, my dusky lad
how will you support a petite maid?
I will make my Zawgyi dance
on a six-gap puppet stage.

Appendix

Public Collections of Burmese Puppets

In Burma, the set of puppets on display in the National Museum in Rangoon dates from the first decades of this century. These have been restored and no longer appear in their original costumes.

In Japan, a set, believed to be modern, exists in the National Museum of Ethnic Cultures, Osaka.

Superb late nineteenth- and early twentieth-century examples can be found in the Staatliche Museum Preussischer Kulturbesitz, Berlin, and at the Hamburgisches Museum Fur Volkerkunde, Hamburg, Germany.

In Britain, rare marionettes (donated by Sir Richard Temple in 1890) can be seen at the Pitt Rivers Museum, Oxford. The Victoria and Albert Museum in London also has some splendid late nineteenth-century puppets. A small number also exists in many of the provincial museums.

Select Bibliography

Ba Han, 'Evolution of Burmese Dramatic Performances and Festive Occasions', *Journal of the Burma Research Society*, Vol. XLIX, No. 1, Rangoon, June 1966.

Crawfurd, J., *Journal of an Embassy from the Governor-General of India to the Court of Ava*, 2 vols., London, 1829.

Dagon Nat Shin, 'Myanmar Yokethay Thabin' [Burmese Puppet Theatre], *Yinkyaihmu*, Rangoon, 1959.

Deedok U Ba Cho, 'Burmese Marionette Stage', *The Chinthe*, Vol. I, Rangoon, 1951.

Epigraphic Birmanica, 'Mon Inscriptions'. *Archaeological Survey of Burma*, Vol. I, Part II, Rangoon, 1960.

Ferrars, Max and Bertha, *Burma*, Sampson Low, Marston and Co., London, 1990.

Fytche, Albert, *Burma Past and Present*, Kegan Paul, London, 1878.

Gordon, C. A., *Our Trip to Burmah*, Bailliere, Tindall and Cox, London, 1875.

Hla Thamein, *Myanmar Yokethay Thabin*, Rangoon, 1968; translated into German by Axfel Bruns, *Brimanische Marionetten*, Berlin, 1990.

————, 'The Burmese Marionette', *Sawaddi*, American Women's Club of Thailand, May–June 1986.

Hmawbee Saya Thein, series of articles entitled 'Pyazat Sar Oak Myar' [Plays in Print], *Thuriya*, Rangoon, c.1930.

Khin Myo Chit, 'Burmese Marionette Theatre', *The Guardian*, Rangoon, 1976.

Marchioness of Dufferin and Ava, *Our Viceregal Life in India*, John Murray, London, 1890.

Maung Htin Aung, *Burmese Drama*, Oxford University Press, 1956.

U Min Naing, 'Preface to Burmese Dance', *Forward*, Rangoon, 1979.

————. *Pyidaungsu Ahka Padaythar* [Dances of the Union of Burma], Ministry of Union Culture, Rangoon, 1959.

Myo Kyaw Aung, 'Burmese Marionettes for Modern Audiences', *Forward*, Vol. VI, December 1967.

Pantanaw Win Thein, 'The Burmese Marionette Theatre', *Forward*, c.1970.

Par Nauk, *Par Nauk e Yokegyi Sin* [Par Nauk's Puppet Stage], Rangoon, 1974.

Pemberton, Captain R. Boileau, 'Journey from Manipoor to Ava, and thence across the Yooma Mountains to Arracan in 1830'; reprinted in *Journal of the Burma Research Society*, Vol. XLIII, Rangoon, 1960.

Sangermano, Vincentius, *The Burmese Empire a Hundred Years Ago*, Archibald Constable & Co. London, 1893.

Shway Yoe (Sir George Scott), *The Burman, His Life and Notions*, Macmillan and Co., London, 1896.

Shwe Wair Aye, 'Thabin Wun Hmattan' [Records of the Thabin Wun], *Ngwe Tar Ye*, Rangoon, 1973.

Symes, Michael, *An Account of an Embassy to the Kingdom of Ava sent by the Governor-General of India in the Year 1795*, London, 1800.

Thakin Kodaw Hmaing, *Galonpyan-dipa-nika*, Rangoon, *c.*1920.

U Thaw Zin, 'Thabin Ah Sa Yokethay Ka' [Dance and Drama Began with Marionettes], *Payphu Hlwar*, Rangoon, *c.*1959.

———, 'Yokethay Pyinna' [The Art of the Puppet Theatre], *Ngwe Tar Ye*, Rangoon, 1976.

U Thein Naing, *Myanmar Yokethay Thabin* [Burmese Puppet Theatre], Rangoon, 1966.

Yule, Henry, *A Narrative of the Mission sent by the Governor-General of India to the Court of Ava in 1855*, London, 1858; reprinted Kuala Lumpur, Oxford University Press, 1968.

Zeya, 'Kabar Yokethay hnin Myanmar Yokethay' [Burmese and Foreign Puppets], *Myawaddy*, Rangoon, 1964.

Over fifty articles and books on puppets are available in the Burmese language.

Index

INDEX